CARE PACKAGE

A PATH TO DEEP HEALING

SYLVESTER MCNUTT III

ISBN: 9780692111550
ISBN-13: 978-0-692-11155-0

Printed in The United States Of America

Editing: Elite Editing
Cover Background: World Of Joonas
Cover Design: Sylvester McNutt III

self-published through
Success Is A Choice

sylvestermcnutt.net

Explored Writings in *Care Package*

A Vulnerable Note to You

This is my most vulnerable book. I believe that I am a happy and healthy person; however, we all have many different layers. We are all just like a fresh onion. My attempt here is to peel back some of the layers that are stopping me from moving forward. I have a few obstacles to overcome. Will I do it? I don't know how long it will take, but I have to at least try. I believe you are reading this because we have a similar goal: to truly heal from pain. And that's the beautiful part of this journey—the part where we admit that we have been through a lot and finally open ourselves up to face our demons. If you've read any of my books before, you may think that I'm always vulnerable, but I promise you that *Care Package* offers a level of vulnerability that I have never reached in any of my other books. I dive into scars, I dive into self, and the introspection and self-reflection here are scary. My purpose for exposing myself is to first heal me and then to offer you relatable words or stories that may help heal you.

I love you. I say that for two reasons. One: getting my words out into the marketplace was a very long and hard process. I lost friendships and jobs over this. I lost my sanity and my former self, and I have given up everything to do this. I am forever grateful for people like you, because without you, I wouldn't be here doing this. As artists, as humans, sometimes we lose sight of what matters most, and that's the people you touch, in my humble opinion. That's the first reason I love you. The second reason I love you is because you're willing to invest in yourself. You're willing to take risks to expand, to heal, to grow your mind, or to see things that are completely opposite of you in order to help you reach your potential. If that's not real love, then I don't know what love is. Now let's talk about the structure of *Care Package*.

I like to write introspectively first and then to you second. The reason for this is because I don't want my text to come off as if I'm taking the role of authority. Oftentimes we look at gurus, writers, preachers, teachers, helpers, and others in positions of power as the be-all and end-all.

I never want you to do that with me or my work. I don't consider myself to be any of those things listed above. In my mind, I am simply an artist. We are two students on a journey together, looking for truth, and I want my writing to look within for me and for you. I do not have answers. This book is not about answers. *Care Package* will not save you. It will not change you, for it is not the power—you are the power. The sole purpose of my words is to shine light on something that is inside of you, to ask you questions, to cause conflict with how you think, to offer words that show a path to finding what you need at that moment. Nothing that I say is truth, valid, or important. I am only a messenger. You are the power, you are the guru, and you are the one.

The excerpts, shorter poems, and tables help me connect to my readers who cannot afford my books like you. I post those for them—for the kid who has no money but uses Twitter to find hope. I post the small excerpt for the woman who wants to kill herself, but doesn't, because she saw my words. For the man who is on the verge of breaking down, I want him to find my words, and I want him to know that it will be okay. I post my words on the internet so I can look back and find the words that I need to maintain my life, stay inspired, or get motivated to create.

I love the art of writing, creating, and sharing thought. This is my seventh book, and I cannot explain to you how humbled I am that people keep reading my work. I will never take it for granted. I wake up every day and focus on expanding my mind, my perspective, and my understanding of the world. I am humbled greatly that people like you spend your hard-earned money to view my content. I will never take your effort for granted, because you spent your hard-earned money on my words, and that inspires me to go as deep as I can, to be as real as I can, and to never be perfect but to be what I am. Thank you for embracing this project. I love you; I appreciate you. I am humbled by you, and I hope we can continue to build our friendship through words. You give my words meaning; you give my words power.

I believe *Care Package* tackles some of the tough issues that prevent us from moving forward— some rooted in childhood, some that occurred during the teen years, and almost all plaguing some, if not all, adults. I believe the outline of this book is perfect for healing. We start off talking about alignment and recognizing that we are off. We shift to walking away from pain and letting go, and then we learn how to set boundaries. The middle of the book focuses on guilt and codependency, which leads us to self-care and putting yourself first. The last few chapters round us out and give us new flesh: overcoming anxiety, living in the moment, continuing to love, and finally healing.

You'll notice that each section could be taught as a curriculum or as a healing process. I created *Care Package* so that it one day could be taught in schools or to people who want true healing. I believe these are topics that we don't talk about enough in our society. *Care Package* is my effort to be the change I want to see in the world. In order to fix anything in business, in sports, in relationship matters, or within we must always start with the observation of alignment. Alignment helps us figure out what pieces of the puzzle are in the wrong places, so let's start there.

ONE

ALIGNMENT

I find it madly ironic that when one thing is out of alignment, an entire project can go wrong. If the NASA engineers are off by one inch, it will result in a fatal catastrophe. If the trajectory of your jump shot is not optimal, you will shoot at a lower rate. If you have the wrong friends, you will produce the wrong results. My friends, alignment is everything.□

How to Identify When
You Are Out of Alignment

I have dealt with back pain for the last two years. Something is not right in my midback area. I played football for ten-plus years. I lift weights and play basketball three times a week.

If you know just a little bit about the human body, you know that these activities cause stress on the body. As far as I understand, stress on the body isn't always a bad thing. If you want to grow your muscles, working out adds a stress that seems to give positive results—stronger muscles. However, all stress isn't good; especially if said stress causes pain, then it is definitely not good.

The pain that I have in my midback causes me a great deal of unbearable stress. I experience restless nights of tossing and turning, and it slows down my day-to-day functionality. It's hidden pain because I never talk about it with friends and family members; plus, you cannot see it since I do not limp. I am very strong physically and mentally, so people who are simply observing me are unable to identify this pain that I deal with. And that's the thing about pain. Sometimes it's on our face as tears, and other times it's hidden deep within. People on the outside have no idea what we're fighting. The only people who know I have back trouble are the doctors whom I've seen. I'm not ashamed of the pain. I just didn't care to openly talk about it until this moment, because it seemed irrelevant. I woke up the other day and could barely move. My neck was tight, my back was throbbing in pain, and my shoulders felt like I had lifted a truck the day before.

I could barely put on a shirt. Instead of feeling sorry for myself and cornering myself into the victim role, where we typically all love to go when we feel pain, I decided to make a plan that would help me abolish the back pain and ultimately give me the proper back *alignment*. The back pain is helping me understand the rest of the world in a way that I have never seen it. It's poetic. Can you see that?

Because of my back pain, my life is not operating on the highest wave possible. I'm dealing with pain every single day, and it's seeping in so deep that it's affecting other activities, like sex, rest, the ability to relax, and my inner peace.

You can look at your life right now and observe something that is out of alignment: your job, your mental health—hell, maybe you have back pain, too, or you have a best friend who is crossing borders and boundaries. No matter what, we all have something in our lives that is simply not aligned the way it should be. Typically, it's something like back pain, something that you don't truly feel like explaining or expressing to everyone.

So I challenge you to do as I've done for myself: list it. Become fully aware of it without putting yourself down. Is it my fault that I have this back pain? Yes. Do I deserve to beat myself up over it? Absolutely not. I want you to understand that most of us add pain on top of pain, and that will never ever solve the problem of pain.

If you want to rid yourself of pain, you have to release the pain bodies, the triggers, or the actual entity that is causing you the burden. For the sake of consistency, I am going to stick to my back-pain analogy, because not only is it true but it's easy to understand and transfer over into your life. It's something that I hope you can take with you and remember as you go through life. I want you to think, "Damn, is my back out of alignment like 2017 Sylvester, or is it aligned like 2018 Sylvester?"

As December 2017 starts, and I have committed to ridding myself of this damn back pain, the first step I took after identifying the pain was to look at what I was doing and what I had already done around this problem. That is step two as far as aligning yourself goes.

What Behaviors Am I Doing Right Now, and What Do I Need to Change?

Most people are unwilling to change. Most people are so stuck in their ways that they'll stop at this first step. Change is hard, and identifying that you are the one messing up your life—not the man, not society, not your husband or wife, but you—is a responsibility that most humans never want to bear. Here's the crazy thing about accepting that you and only you have ruined your life: it gives you power.

The fact is that you and only you can fix it. It's understanding and accepting that you have always had the power deep inside of you, but because of your thoughts, you have never empowered yourself enough to feel like you have the power. The next step toward aligning yourself correctly is to make a new plan. The best way to make a plan is to layer it. You want to have short-range, midrange, and long-range goals inside of the plan. Allow yourself space to adjust the plan as you go. Having a rigid plan forces you to remain one way, when the pain itself is there to help you grow. Sometimes we outgrow plans and the pace of the plan, and the only way to ensure that you do not trap yourself is to remain completely fluid and agile throughout the plan. The final step toward fixing the alignment is to listen to your body and your mind and to observe how your life changes after you start executing the plan.

Back to my back. You already know that I am dealing with an immense amount of pain, so the next question is, What did I do, or what am I doing, to rid myself of it? Following the steps that I just gave you, the first thing I did was realize that I needed to sleep more. I realized that I needed to play basketball at least one day less per week because the stress on my joints is no longer beneficial to me. I have decided that I am committing to acupuncture and cupping for the remainder of the year while also adding two yoga sessions per week. I've done yoga before, and I've done acupuncture. I am aware of the healing properties of both, but what I needed was a commitment to it as well as the subtraction of something that I enjoy. Right now three days a week of full-court basketball could be having a negative impact. Many people are not willing to stop doing what they've been doing even though they are the ones who claim they want to change. Funny how that works out. I made my commitment to a new plan, one that feels like it will give me new results, and if it doesn't work, that's okay—at least I was willing to try something different.

When you feel like you are out of alignment, that is your body, your mind, your heart, and your intuition telling you that you must adjust. Do not be the type of person who ignores the inner dialogue. That's like punching yourself in the face during winter while you're walking blindfolded down a one-way street. If you ignore yourself, you will have an accident, and it won't be pretty. On the next page, I've listed these steps for people who enjoy numbers and bullet points.

☐

☐

☐

☐

☐

☐

☐

☐

☐

☐

☐

☐

☐

☐

☐

Four Ways To Realign Your Life

1. Identify the problem.
2. Become fully aware of what you've done to cause it and what you're doing to fix it.
3. Make a new, flexible plan to attack the problem.
4. Listen to yourself and observe your life as you execute the plan.

Sometimes pain is
on our face as tears,
and other times it's
hidden deep within,
and people on the
outside have no idea
what we're fighting.

—s. mcnutt

When you feel pain,
don't hide it. Pain is
like garbage. You may
not see it, but you'll
know it's there until
you throw it out.

—s. mcnutt□

Nothing stays the
same. Be willing
to grow, to learn,
to transform. Be
like the phoenix.

—s. mcnutt

Your ability to align
your life correctly is
not determined by
other people.

—s. mcnutt□

The only way to
be sane is to leave
behind the insane
people and places
you visit now.

—s. mcnutt

Life will give you a
hundred reasons to
cry, but the fact that
you still have a
heartbeat is your
thousand reasons to
smile and laugh.

—s. mcnutt☐

When things go
wrong in your life,
you have to focus
on getting stronger.

—s. mcnutt

Getting stronger
doesn't mean acting
like you have it
all together.
Strength is also
allowing certain
things to fall apart.

—s. mcnutt□

When nega
finds you, r
back. If yo
become it.

—s. mcnutt

As you grow, the
people you knew
will start to feel like
strangers if they do
not grow with you.

—s. mcnutt□

Put yourself in
a situation that
makes you happy.

—s. mcnutt

Never be rigid.
The wind flows;
it moves around
objects no matter
what; be able to
flow like the wind.

—s. mcnutt□

If you have
to break a
commitment
to keep your
life aligned,
do it.

—s. mcnutt

Nowadays, we want
things to happen so
fast. Slow down;
trust the process.

—s. mcnutt □

If a train goes
too fast, it could
easily derail.

Don't assume
you need
to give up
when you run
into problems.

Sometimes
you're just
going too fast,
or you want it
to happen
too quickly.

Slow down.
Allow things
to play out slower,
without force,
without control.

— s. mcnutt☐

Fact: obsessive
overthinking never
helps you. Let it be
what it will be. Let it
flow naturally.

—s. mcnutt□

You're always at
work. Make sure
the job aligns with
your core values.

—s. mcnutt□

Three Tips That Will Help You Pick the Right Job

All across the world, we tell our friends the same thing: do something you love. You know what's funny about that? It's always people who do not do what they love who are telling other people to do what they love. I'm not going to give you that cookie-cutter advice for three reasons: One, that's not useful information. Two, you might not know what you love, and three, you might be doing what needs to be done for survival, and I'm never going to judge you for that. These three tips will help you pick the right job when the time is right.

One: Try a bunch of things when you are younger. It's amazing to me how we expect eighteen-year-old kids to know their majors, what their lives will be, and to be set on this "plan." I know people in their thirties and forties who have no clue what they're doing, yet we expect kids to know, and that expectation is foolish. The best thing I did with my life was attempt a bunch of different things until I figured out what I liked. Don't think this is limited to just jobs either. You should be trying different activities, foods, and different people too. *Disclaimer*: If you jump from job to job every four to six months, it will look like you do not understand commitment, and this could hinder the hiring process. Be very methodical in your approach to leaving jobs.

Two: Get what you're worth. This is a paradox because there are times you have to go through a situation that actually helps you get what you're worth, and other times you have to stay to a point where you realize, *Damn, I'm not getting treated the way I deserve.* You must always have an open mind. Knowing your worth is about knowing what you can contribute and also knowing what you're not willing to take or settle for.

I left a really "good" job because I didn't feel like I was getting what I was worth. Most people are unwilling to quit a $60,000–$70,000 per year job. I knew I was worth more than that. I knew I could make that amount in a month. I knew that I could double or triple that yearly salary, but I also knew that I needed the job to help me build it. I stayed at my job and built my business on the side. Most people are unwilling to do that much work. Most people claim they're worth more, but they are lazy and unfocused. If you feel like you deserve more, there are two things that you must have at all times to create the success you want: *vision* and *drive*. In the example I gave you, keep in mind that maximizing my income was a priority, and it was directly connected to my "worth."

Three: There is value in taking a lower-paying job if it will bring you happiness; however, there is value in giving yourself more security with the higher-paying job. Looking for higher pay or looking for what you love may not be what's best for you. You may have to combine the two. This is where a lot of people get lost. They don't know if they should do what they love or if they should secure the bag. I am a person who does what he loves for a living, which is to create content daily, write my books, create videos, and do public speaking. It is important to note that I was doing it for free before I was doing it for pay. It is important to note that I went to college for it and knew that I wanted to do this in high school. Most people don't know what they want to do, and that is why they suffer. Most people don't invest in learning, in education, in experience, in *what they love*. In my specific situation, I always knew what I wanted to do. I just didn't know how I was going to create it as a job, and so I just did it for free. I did it for free until people decided to pay me for products, services, ideas, and my time, and then I had to figure out how to multiply it so it could be consistent. Don't get caught up in looking for a job you love or a job that pays more—that will fail you. I truly believe the smartest thing you can do is consistently evaluate what's going on in your life, make a plan for what you want, and then take massive action to create it. It's a process, not a light switch, so you have to be patient with the process.□

Suspend ego;
pause, observe the
energy around you,
understand, and
listen more than
you speak.

—s. mcnutt☐

There is value in
taking a lower-paying
job if it will bring a
higher amount of
happiness.
—s. mcnutt☐

I wish I could make everyone understand how important this statement is: *go where you are wanted*.

—s. mcnutt

The right friends will challenge you to do better. They'll see greatness inside of you before you do.

—s. mcnutt□

Three Important Tricks That Will Help You Pick the Right Friends

1. *Become fully aware of their goals, their ambitions, and the actions they're currently taking to manifest the life that they claim they want.*

   They always say that your life is similar to the five people you interact with most, and if that is true for you, it is important that your friends somewhat align with your goals and ambitions. Of course, respect that everyone is on their own path and time line, but this still matters.

2. *Ask them probing questions about how they feel about pain, love, and what success looks like to them.*

   Aligning yourself with the right friends will save you from pain and can introduce you to love or success.

3. *Figure out quickly if they're the type of people who will be honest with you.* □

   Why? Because you need people whom you can trust, who can give you an honest perception of how you behave. Honest friends help sharpen you, they help inspire you, they help you see yourself without your ego.□

Break up with the
friends who are full
of ego and pride,
friends who claim
to do no wrong.

—s. mcnutt

I no longer chase
anything or anyone.
I work for what I
want and remain
patient while going
after it.

—s. mcnutt☐

Powerful Friendships Do This:

- Challenge you to grow

- Listen to your shortcomings

- Provide realistic feedback about your skill sets and abilities.

- Fulfill hierarchal need for human connection.

- Learn and share personal interests.

- Have dialogue about intimate relationships to gain perspective or confirmation.

- Engage in mostly fun and enjoyable environments.

- Provide support mentally or emotionally through diverse life moments.

TWO

WALKING AWAY FROM PAIN

There are too many adults walking around with pain that has never been talked about. We mask it, we hide it, we keep it in the closet because we are afraid to wear the outfits of pain.□

This time in my
life is dedicated
to healing deeply,
while attracting
happiness.

—s. mcnutt

Be completely
aware of your pain,
but don't allow it to
define who you are.
Pain is an emotion
that passes.

—s. mcnutt□

Healing Is Not Complex; It Is Simple

No matter what, always remember this: *healing is a choice*. And once you decide to heal, you will. The last time I wrote about pain in one of my books was about four years ago. In my book *Dear Soul: Love After Pain*, I wrote deeply about all types of pain—how to get through it and how to manage it. In the time that has passed, I haven't experienced very much pain. Some, yes, but I've done a great job of managing the pain that I have experienced, and that is all I want to do with *Care Package*. I want to deliver words, ideas, and strategies that will help you manage new pain as it comes into your life.

Before that book, I lost a relationship, my father, my job, and my identity, and I was in a place of rebuilding. I wrote the book to myself as a way to heal, to face some of the things from my childhood that I dealt with in order to let them go.

Some of my fans have said that my books heal them, and I am grateful for that, but I would never call myself a spiritual healer. Maybe I am one, and I am just in denial. Who knows? I don't have the answer to that question, nor do I need it. I feel like *Care Package* is helping me heal some different pains. I've had to deal with guilt, shame, and codependency, and to be completely honest, the guilt eats me alive. My purpose for writing *Care Package* to myself is to eliminate all this guilt that I have, because I know that I do not deserve it.

Pain is hard for most people because we define ourselves as pain. We see ourselves as the stories of our past. We lock pain into our minds because we identify with those stories. We judge ourselves in the present moment based on what we experienced before, and we constantly preach to ourselves a level of unworthiness. We take aggressive positions toward our past, cursing at our exes, damning our parents, and holding on to resentment toward an irrelevant person who hurt our feelings years and years ago. All this suffering exists because we lock it into our egos. We lock it into the sense of "me."

My solution for this is to change the narrative. Stop making abuse, pain, and neglect your story. Simply acknowledge that it is a story that you experienced. Literally changing your inner dialogue from *This is what happened to me* to *Here is what I learned from this situation* will change how the stories of your past feel.

Healing is a process that starts, occurs, and ends in your mind. Your brain is a tool. If you have used this tool incorrectly in the past, I hope we can change it moving forward. Let's talk deeper about locking pain into your mind and how we can undo it —how we can free the ego and that pain.

Locking Pain into Your Mind☐
☐

We suffer greatly because we don't understand our minds, the words we use, or how we associate with and deal with pain. The first step toward healing from pain is to become completely aware of how you choose to associate with pain. Look at the differences between these two sets of statements:

"I went through a lot when I was younger."
"Nobody cared about me when I was younger."

or

"Why does this always happen to me?"
"What can I learn about this situation?"

Simply altering and manipulating the words you use can literally change how your mind associates with pain. I don't care to identify with my past pain, but I also don't think it's healthy to dismiss it and act like it never occurred. I'll give you an example to illustrate what I am saying here. My father and mother had no issue with spankings and whippings as a way to discipline me and my siblings. Personally, I never felt like it did anything other than instill hate and fear inside me. As a result, I was a child who didn't feel loved, didn't feel like I could speak my mind, and never cared to have dialogue with anyone, because I was conditioned to think that people would hurt me if they didn't like what I said or if my behavior didn't align with what they wanted. Of course, I had to heal and unlearn from that pain, but for a while I suffered because I chose to identify with the pain. I didn't accept what I told you earlier: *healing is a choice*. Now that I know healing is a choice, I can heal from the childhood pain and conditioning that my mind has identified with. You're going to ask me how I healed from the childhood trauma, so let's go deeper.

Process to Heal from Childhood Pain

1. Stop identifying with the pain. The pain is in the past. It is something that happened; it is not something that is happening.
2. Realize that you have to forgive the people who *caused* you the pain even if you don't want to.
3. Learn the psychology about how your childhood traumas have affected you as an adult (e.g., fear, abuse, and abandonment). Do the research to

figure out the end results of such treatment so you can know how it affects you today. If the research is too hard, seek therapy and counseling to uncover those answers with a professional—it will help.

4. Learn that living in the present moment will always heal you. Living in the past forces you to align with it, especially if there is pain. Living in the future forces you to be anxious—live here.

Freedom from Pain

Once you are able to fully see through your consciousness that you have been locking pain into your mind, then and only then will you unlock it. I gave you an example above about the type of language that haunts you and fixates you into the abyss of pain. Do you want to suffer, or do you want to be free? When you change those words to "What can I learn about this situation?" then the entire situation changes. You just placed yourself in the presence of power, in the presence of healing, and this why healing is a choice. You have the choice to change your words, which changes your outlook and as a result changes your life. I want to go a little bit deeper with locking pain into your mind. Paying attention to the words you use has the power to one of do two things: *free you* or *enslave you*. Enslavement is the pain on the face of animals at the zoo. Freedom is when you watch sports and you watch the winning team win the championship. Which do you want? Which do you deserve? I know for a fact you're going to say that you want freedom from pain, but do you believe that? Do you genuinely, in the bottom of your heart, believe that you deserve that? Once you answer that question, a million pounds of pressure will be lifted from your soul.

Pain Is a Cycle
Until You Break It

When I was a young boy, I was always getting into fights with other boys. This makes sense, considering that I was raised in a violent household and a violent environment. I became silent because it was normalized in that area. It was a cycle of pain —at lunch, after school, before school, with my brothers, and with my dad. With the childlike consciousness, I couldn't tell you why then, but I can now. There was pain that lived inside of me. Eckhart Tolle refers to them as pain bodies in his book *The Power of Now*. When you have a pain body, it's like a heat-seeking missile that has been launched from a plane. Its sole mission is to search for pain—to find a host, a target who will help keep it alive. To search for pain inside of other people. To find people who will meet this pain and welcome it.

The reason you have toxic relationships over and over again is because you've never healed the pain, and the pain lives inside of you. As a result of never dealing with the pain, it attracts people who can continue the cycle of pain. That's why it was so easy for me to fight boys, to argue with teachers, and to talk crazy to my parents when I was younger because the pain was given to me. And, of course, I was an innocent child, so I had no idea what was going on. I took the pain. I became a host for the pain. I accepted the pain and helped it grow because I searched for other pain bodies. So the question I have to ask you is this: *How much longer can you continue to repeat these cycles of pain?* When are you going to change the way your life is going? And the most important question that you must have for yourself is this: *Is it possible that I can stop the cycles, starting with my behavior and my perspectives?*

In my experience, starting with these questions will be the foundation of resolution. Once I accepted that it was possible for me to change, that I deserved more, and that I did not want to suffer, that is when my life changed for the better. That is when

I had a spiritual awakening. I realized that I did not need to fight anyone. I realized that I could have a peaceful life, and most importantly, I realized that I deserved it. It was my duty to deliver this to myself. Please take an inventory of your life. Look at the last six or seven years and just observe the interactions—the friendships, the dating partners—and become fully aware of the full spectrum of how things went. Become aware of what you brought to the madness. Become aware of it all, but do not label or judge yourself. Do not label them. This exercise is not done because you need to place blame; it's done to increase awareness so you can rise and create a new life. That's it. Blame is not important to me. If you're going to blame anyone, blame yourself, because blaming yourself will give you the power to fix it. But for the purpose of this exercise, do not blame—just become aware. Over the next few pages, I'd like to address why you need to be aware of your pain without judging or blaming anyone for the pain and how being aware of your pain, in a way, may free you from it.

Healing from pain is a choice. You have to consciously decide that you deserve to feel free, that you deserve to let go of the weight that has been holding you down for too long.

—s. mcnutt □

Break up with the mind-set that you have haters—that people are against you, that you have enemies.

—s. mcnutt □

Thinking you have
haters will manifest
low-vibrational
energy. Instead, think
about true friendships
and genuine energy.
That's how you use
the universe to attract
powerful allies.

—s. mcnutt □
□
□
□

A truly aware person
understands the power
of thoughts and never
has the me-against-
the-world mind-set.
Thinking people are
against you will
isolate you; it will
hurt you more. Trust
and know that there
are good people who
want to bring you
positive energy.

—s. mcnutt □

Destroying the Me-against-the-World Mind-Set

My entire mind-set switched for the better when I abolished the me-against-the-world mind-set. I grew up with the me-against-the-world mind-set because of my pain. I felt like everyone wanted to hurt me because people in the past have. I did what most adults do, which is carry the pain. *Therapists refer to it as survivor's mind-set*. When you feel like you've been abandoned and left for dead, and nobody wants you, defeating the odds makes you a survivor; it makes you a warrior. When you've been abandoned emotionally, you develop strength within, but you also don't let people get close to you. You try your best to keep evil energy out, but a mask comes over you because you often judge other people wrong or develop a victim mentality. Why do you develop these walls and become jaded? Because you feel like people will leave once you let them in, or they will come in just to hurt you. These thoughts are normal; we are just protecting ourselves. It's called self-preservation. I knew I needed to grow out of the extreme paranoia, and I did, and if you have that, you will too. Just be patient reading *Care Package* and be patient with yourself, and you'll slowly alleviate it.

That's what happened to me, and I knew I

needed to grow out of the me-against-the-world mind-set. Later, in my twenties, I had a spiritual awakening. I realized that there's no such thing as an enemy or a hater. It may sound crazy, and that's okay because *I am crazy*, but I feel like I don't have any opponents in life. Mind you, I grew up playing football. I played in college, and I played arena football. I'm supercompetitive, but after my spiritual awakening, I realized that I do not have any opponents. I realized that the only opponent I'll ever have in life is my mind. When I have inner conflict, that causes me more pain than any other person is possible of causing. People are not bad. People are not out to get you. People genuinely don't go around trying to hurt others. Let's not be naïve. Of course there are bad people, and there are even good people who do bad things. We know that. We are not delusional to the fact that some human beings' behavior is disgusting. But I cannot operate at a frequency where I walk around thinking the worst of every single human being. That is a pessimistic state that I don't want to live in, one filled with depression, anxiety, and paranoia.

The life of paranoia is uneasy. It feels like hell to think everyone is going to attack you. And if you truly sit back, observe, and look at reality, you'll see that there have been more people in your life who have caused you no harm versus the very few who have caused you harm.

In life, you have
already gone through
the worst. It made you
stronger, and now you
are ready for the best.
—s. mcnutt

You will overcome
what you are fighting
through, you will find
inner-peace, and one
day this struggle
won't feel as strong as
it does now. Be patient
and keep working
towards healing.
- s.mcnutt☐

When you've been
abandoned, you
develop strength within,
but you also don't let
people get close to you.

—s. mcnutt☐

Being aware of your
perspective matters. If
you believe the world is
against you, it will be. If
you believe the world is
here for you, it will be.

—s. mcnutt☐

Focus on your lane—
on your life—and put
energy into making
your life better.

—s. mcnutt☐

A person will
continue to have
toxic connections for
two reasons: they
have not healed from
the pain of previous
relationships, and
they don't know
how to set healthy
boundaries.

—s. mcnutt☐

When we go through
madness, it feels like
it will last forever,
but nothing is forever.
The pain is temporary
too. It will fade.

—s. mcnutt

I have forgiven everyone
who has caused me pain.
Most of them haven't
apologized. I'm forgiving
them because my healing
is more important than
me holding a grudge,
which is more suffering.

—s. mcnutt□

Healing looks like
forgiving people
who have never
apologized—people
who see no harm
with what they
have done.

—s. mcnutt

Pain trapped me.
Once I forgave
the people who
hurt me, I became
a free soul.

—s. mcnutt

Telling myself
this has helped
me forgive with
compassion:

"They did the best
they could with
what they had."

—s. mcnutt

Before you get in a new
relationship make sure
you are healed from the
last one.

—s. mcnutt□

Delete numbers out
of your phone, detox
your time line, change
your routine. Do what
needs to be done so
you can save yourself.

—s. mcnutt

☐
☐
☐
☐
☐
☐
☐
☐
☐
☐

The pain that came
to you is not always
a choice, but keeping
it on you is. Forgive.
Stop the obsessive
thinking related to it,
and allow the pain to
fade away.

—s. mcnutt☐

Learning to Forgive
So You Can Heal

Bitter people will say that the person who hurt them doesn't deserve to be forgiven. If you believe that, you will suffer forever just like they do. It will not be easy to forgive people. We do not practice forgiveness; we practice holding on to pain. We practice reinforcing our egos, and that traps the pain and keeps the cycle going. Forgiveness is the key to breaking the chains of pain that stay locked around your neck. First you have to stop living with your sense of entitlement. You feel like the world owes you everything—every explanation and every action should be in your favor. That's laughable at best. Keeping that mind-set will forever enslave you with your pain. Once you accept that nobody owes you anything, which is you freeing your ego, then you can forgive the people who have hurt you. Holding on to pain is a choice, and once you choose to heal, you choose to forgive the people who brought you the pain. This is a process, not a light switch. It is hard because it is the opposite of what we have been taught. Be ready for the challenge— you can do it.

Do you want to stay bitter and hurt, or do you want to heal? Which choice are you going to make? If you forgive your ex, your parent, or even yourself, then you allow the pain to live in the past.

Forgiveness allows you to separate the past from the present. Many people do not heal in the now, because they are too identified with the past. They care too much about the story they tell themselves about who they are. The easiest way to ruin your life is to tell yourself stories about the past, to believe these stories, and to box yourself into what those stories tell you about who you are or who you can be.

In the story I gave you, I shared some of the pain I dealt with growing up. I told you how I choose to forgive. I told you how I choose to seek therapy and counseling to help me understand that type of treatment so I can grow from it. Now I do not identify with the pain of the past. I have chosen to forgive my father, my mother, and any person whom I've known from my past. I don't buy in to self-defeating thoughts about what I can't do, how I'm disadvantaged, or how I am less of a person because of some pain I experienced many years ago. What I just explained to you is the perfect example of why I don't suffer. I don't identify with the pain. It is not locked in my mind. You do not have to suffer either; you do not have to lock it into your mind.

Learning to forgive is a process, but it's easier

for you to do once you get out of your ego and get out of your mind.

Healing is a
process, not
a light switch.
Don't feel like
you will heal
in one day,
for most of it
takes years.

—s. mcnutt

Allow your healing
process to flow at
the organic pace it
deserves. You cannot
rush or expect to be
over pain instantly,
it takes time. Be patient
with yourself and trust
that it will get better.

—s. mcnutt☐

Forgiving someone
doesn't mean you're
allowing them to
come back. It means
you're choosing to let
go of the pain they
once brought.

—s. mcnutt

Pain has a stickiness
factor. You don't want
it to stay on you like a
scent. You want it to
go. Be willing to
detox, to shed dead
weight, to let go of
irrelevant energy.

—s. mcnutt□

Choose your words
wisely. Words can
be forgiven, but the
impact they have
may not be forgotten.

—s. mcnutt

A Letter to Pain

Hey, pain, I've gotten to know
you well at different parts of my
life, and as much as I want to be
angry with you, I have to thank
you. You taught me how to grow,
how to learn who I am, and most
importantly, you taught me how
to avoid you. I am grateful for
the people you have brought me.
I am also sorry because I have
hurt people too. I hope I can be
forgiven for my ways, for the
pain that I have caused too.

—s. mcnutt☐

In order to heal, we
have to be aware of
the pain we have
caused other people.
We have to be willing
to apologize and be
accountable for it.

—s. mcnutt☐

On Forgiveness

Most people will suffer for
the rest of their lives because
they're too proud to forgive
people who have hurt them.
They say things like, "This
person doesn't deserve
forgiveness." The second that
you are able to forgive them
for what they've done is the
second that you open a
lifetime of healing and peace.

—s. mcnutt☐

Healing

We heal more when
we do not allow our
emotions to explode
out of control.

The key: learn what
and who triggers you,
and then practice the
art of pausing,
breathing deeply, and
allowing the outburst
to pass.

—s. mcnutt

Cultivate a Healthy Relationship

Create a flowing, open,
and judgment-free
dialogue. It's not always
about having answers.
It's truly about having a
conversation. Cultivate a
space where both people
can be unmasked.

—s. mcnutt □

Cultivate a Healthy Relationship

Use a healthy tone of voice, make eye contact, and avoid the nonverbal cues that show anger or hostility.

—s. mcnutt□

One of the worst mistakes you can make is to greet your partner with aggressive, upset, unruly energy.

If there is an issue, breathe, relax, and approach them with compassion.

—s. mcnutt□

Protecting the Sacred
Greeting and Exit

I am the child of divorced parents. My parents split when I was fourteen for the last time. They did the fake breakup at least four times. The first six to eight years of my life, my parents were happy and did a great job creating our family. I remember walks in the park, parties, movie nights, and bonding over cards and conversation. I was younger, but I was still a hyperaware child, and I didn't feel, nor do I remember, too many vibes that were *off*.

Between the ages of eight and twelve, everything changed. My parents worked so much that when they came home they were so tired. They had nothing left to give. They had nothing to give us children or each other. Eventually, they just became roommates and stopped greeting each other. There was no excitement when someone came home. We didn't honor anyone anymore. Previously, we used to honor each other when someone left or came back. You know how small children are—always excited when people come around whom they like. That childlike spirit that we had in the house began to vanish.

One of the best strategies you can implement in your relationship is to make coming home and leaving home a sacred ritual. Make it a process of honoring the new person or new energy.

Maybe it means the person who comes home walks into a hug and a kiss on the cheek. Maybe there's a signature handshake. Maybe you're a fit family, and you make each other do three push-ups. We all say now that this may be silly or too much, but if you've ever lost someone before, then you know the only thing we ask for when we lose someone is more time. No matter what, try to protect the greeting and the exit. This part of the daily interactions is sacred. Please cherish it. You never know when it will be the last time you see someone. Make sure the last thought of you is welcome and warm, loving and kind.☐

What you're unwilling
to do for your partner,
another person will.
Focus on learning your
partner's wants and needs
as well as expressing
yours. Do not avoid this.

—s. mcnutt

You should often ask
your partner to express
their needs to you. If
they don't tell you,
how can you help
fulfill their experience?
This goes both ways.

—s. mcnutt□

The emotion of love isn't enough to keep two people together. There has to be communication, compatibility, understanding, and most importantly, there has to be desire on both ends to keep adding value to each other's existence.

—s. mcnutt

Make sure you always show love towards the people you care about. Life does a great job of making us mad, making us focus on work, and school. I implore you to focus on love, to focus on giving value to those you care about.

—s. mcnutt □

How to Stop Being Triggered

It is imperative that you deal with your past traumas and pains. If not, you will often operate with some of the most destructive emotions: fear, rage, anxiety, shame, guilt, panic, paranoia, and others.

A healthy adult employs reason and logic, not to the point of going cold and lacking emotion but in conjunction with emotion. Emotion is not bad; it is necessary. But living without control due to emotional spikes can be catastrophic, meaning that relationships can end in a split second because one person can't control his or her behavior or reaction to situations.

As an adult, it is your duty to yourself, to your friends, and to your coworkers to learn how to manage your emotions. I'm not saying act like they're not there. I am saying evolve to a point where you can suppress your ego, your fears, and the primal negative motivators that make you act like a child when you do not get your way. This is a tough pill to swallow, but a very necessary one.

The best advice you'll ever receive on how to manage your emotions is to breathe. Everything about your emotions revolves around how you breathe and your inner dialogue. The next time you lose control, tell yourself to breathe. That is you taking control of your inner dialogue and your emotions.

When you feel yourself becoming triggered, do not ball up your fist. Do not scream and yell at the top of your lungs. Do not fight to be heard. It is possible that the other people around you do not have big enough ears to understand where you're coming from. Do not bicker and make comments under your breath. Do not attack or put them down. Do not throw your alarm clock through the wall, and if you're wondering, I may or may not have done that one time in college. This is my formal apology to my roommates and to the apartment complex for the hole. And to answer your question, yes, we left the alarm clock in the hole, and it hung there all year. If you went away for college, this doesn't surprise you—you've seen worse.

At the end of the day, overreacting will never make the situation better, so it is our goal to understand that before we act. The next time you become super triggered and unruly, make sure you pause, breathe, and gather yourself when these primal negative emotions take control. This happens to every person, but the most efficient thing to do, in my opinion is to practice controlling it, and that doesn't mean you have it mastered by midnight tonight. Practice means you take a conscious effort to get better at something through repetition, through coaching, through adjusting. Here is a practice that will help you tremendously on your journey. You have to give yourself at least three to five seconds of pure relaxation before you respond to some things, and if you say these words in bold slowly, aloud if possible, this practice will change your life. I have been saying this to myself for ten years, and each year it gets easier and easier to let things go, to never give your power away. Tell yourself these words: **pause, breathe, and relax.**

You will continue to suffer if you have an emotional reaction to everything that is said to you.

True power is sitting back and observing everything with logic; true power is restraint.

If words control you, that means everyone else can control you; breathe and allow things to pass.

—s. mcnutt

You make your life
hard by always being
in your head. Life is
simple, get out of
your head and get into
the moment.

—s. mcnutt

Most people never
heal, because they
stay in their heads,
replaying corrupted
scenarios. Let it go.

—s. mcnutt☐

Sad, broken, depressed. I've had the thoughts that run through your head like a race. "I'm unworthy." I decided that I didn't want to be sad. I decided that I no longer deserved to suffer. I realized that I am worthy of joy, of bliss, of happiness, and so are you. I cried until I ran out of tears, and then I picked myself up. I put myself back together. I fought for myself. I'm not stronger than you. We have the same stories; we are just on two different pages. Fight through this chapter and *walk away from the pain*. You will overcome these pages. Trust me, the story turns beautiful after the ugly.

—s. mcnutt

THREE

LETTING GO

Learning how to let go is a skill. ☐

Letting Go: The Final Step
Toward Healing from Pain

The final step, and what most people will tell you is the hardest step, of healing from pain is the step called letting go. I hope that I have provided enough value already around understanding, identifying, and reflecting on where the pain comes from and why we hold on. I hope some of the value I gave you around dealing with pain has already helped you let go, and my genuine hope is that this section truly helps you with the closure process that you are craving.

In 2014 my father passed away. He was young, only fifty-one at the time. In my opinion, that is way too early to die. I talked in detail about the way he raised me and how it gave me pain and trauma, and I don't write these words in vain or to throw shade on someone's legacy. I respect every single person I write about. I am very grateful for my experiences with him and my mother, two people who caused me a great deal of pain. But like I told you in the last chapter, *they did the best they could with what they had, and they tried their best to provide love*. And that is why I choose to forgive them. My father and I did not speak for about five years during my college days, but let me tell you the story why. One summer I was attempting to leave the kitchen, and he demanded that I wash the dishes. I didn't feel like I needed to because they weren't my dishes. They were the dishes from him and his girlfriend, and I didn't feel like I should be responsible for their mess, because I wasn't there to create it. I was working full time at the Home Depot in Palatine, Illinois. I trained at my high-school gym when I wasn't at work since it was across the street. I read books in my spare time, and, of course, I played some PlayStation because I was, and still am, a video-game nerd.

At the time I felt like my life was very simple and organized. I was finally stepping out into my own realm of finding myself, as they say. I told him that I didn't feel like I was responsible for the dishes, because I wasn't home. It wasn't my mess, and I didn't feel like I should be given busywork just because I was the child. I was nineteen years old. Of course, anyone who is a parent may feel some entitlement, and you may align with my father. I understand. In this moment, his ego ran him, and he attacked me with a frying pan, demanding that I wash the dishes. Of course, I defended myself, and he said that if I didn't wash the dishes, I had to leave the house immediately.

What do you think I did? I did exactly what you think I would do, exactly what I preach. I packed my bag and left because I realized my worth. I realized that regardless of our relationship, nobody had the right to treat me like that, attack me, or threaten me physically. No human being deserves to fight me, hurt me, or cause me bodily harm. I realized in that moment that nothing could destroy me, because I chose myself over this fake sense of security. I chose myself over family, over what was called love, but that wasn't love. It was one of the first moments in my life where I took control and power away from other people. It was scary, and it was not easy, but I had to choose my own happiness over everything.

That was a fucked-up moment in time, and again, I am still not mad at my father, because he did the best he could with what he had. His life was going down step by step, and just like a ship out to sea with a small hole in it, eventually the water will fill the vessel. If you do not patch the holes, eventually you will sink. *My father put me out.* That is one way you can look at it, and when I was that age I played the victim role, for sure. I told the story like he put me out. But now, with this consciousness that I have, I know the truth, and the truth is that *I put myself out.*

I didn't want my ship to sink like my father's. I didn't want to be unhappy like he was at the time.

He had pain bodies inside of him that he never managed, and his behavior proved it. His behavior looked for other pain bodies, and even though I usually met him in that space, on this day I decided that those pain bodies would no longer have permission to participate in my experience called life.

So What Happened Next?

This was the first time that I was homeless. I wasn't sure what to do, actually. I had no plan, no savings. I had just gotten my first cell phone. I didn't have a car. I was filled with anger and rage because I thought to myself, "What type of parent puts his kid out on the street?" I went to the high school that I attended, and I sat outside. It was the summertime, and nobody was there. I went to this familiar place, and I took in several breaths. I surveyed the land, and for the first time in my life I felt free. This moment of chaos for other people brought me calm and peace. It brought me understanding and serenity. This moment of being homeless and formless brought a smile to my face. I remember saying to myself, "What am I going to do now?" I didn't obsess about going back. I didn't care to apologize, because I genuinely didn't feel like I had done anything wrong. I didn't care to backtrack at all. I only wanted to move forward. I feel like a lot of people go wrong when chaos happens in their lives because they're rigid. They obsess about going backward, forcing what is broken, and it never works. I embrace the chaos. I believe in staying fluid and adaptable. I never try to change what is happening. I accept reality, and I use my skills to adapt.

Eventually, I got a hold of one of my teammates who found out that I was in this situation. His parents agreed to let me stay with them for the summer. I was very grateful for their hospitality and gratitude. They never asked me for anything other than to respect their house rules, and, of course, I did everything that was asked of me.

So let's conclude this here. To be completely vulnerable and honest, this situation brought me a lot of pain. It made me resent and hate my father. It made me develop survivor's mind-set. I developed a certain level of self-reliability because I never wanted to be in a situation like that again. This moment in my life caused me to truly care about making money, to learn how systems like renting an apartment or buying a house worked, and to figure out how to network with people. This very bad situation brought me so many great tools and some unruly inner emotions. I held on to the pain for years. I hated my father and chose not to speak to him for at least five years.

This next part is very important for your life. By not talking to him, what I thought I was doing was separating myself from pain, and I was. To me he was a representation of pain. I feared him. I feared dealing with him because he brought emotions out of me that made me uncomfortable. What I didn't know at the time was how deep my pain bodies were. I didn't know at that time that I was holding on to anger, resentment, fear, disdain, and a victim mind-set. And one day someone said this to me: "*Sylvester, your father is not going to be around forever. You need to forgive him for what he did to you, and you need to move on.*"

To this day I cannot remember who said it. In fact, it's either one of two people, or both of them, who said it. It was either my girlfriend at the time or my auntie Syl, short for Sylvia. I was open to receiving the message. I had matured because for the five years during that time whenever his name came up, it triggered me. Whenever someone talked about our relationship, I shut down and refused to talk. Again, this is how pain makes you act, especially when you decide that you don't want to deal with it.

Finally, I decided that I was going to call him, and he answered. I told him how he made me feel, how he hurt me, and most importantly, I set a boundary. I set a boundary for how I would be treated moving forward. I told him that if he couldn't meet me in this new space with new behaviors, then this would be the first and last conversation with me as a young adult. I was only twenty-three when we had this conversation. We stopped talking when I was nineteen. He reduced the ego that he had five years earlier, and he apologized. He accepted that he could've handled things differently, and he was open to starting a new relationship with me. I know for a fact that he was dealing with guilt and shame, and he felt like he had abused me. Although he never said it, I could feel the shame that he was dealing with, just like he could feel the anger that I was dealing with. That phone conversation gave us healing.

We were both able to let go of the past, and this allowed us to move forward. In my situation, I was fortunate to have what I call a *closure conversation*. However, I do have a very important asterisk. Do not—I repeat, do not—read what I just said and think that is your signal to call someone who abused you, who beat you, who caused you bodily harm. Do not. In fact, if it was that serious, it's best that you stay away. I feel fortunate that I had a forgiving person who was willing to change. I also developed an unreal level of strength through my weight training and mental strength through my spiritual awakening. I no longer felt like he, or anyone for that matter, could harm me, and that is part of why I decided to rekindle our relationship. I know my fans take my words very literally, and I hope you see that I am simply telling you a story about my life—about what I went through, about how I felt, about what I decided to do. If I didn't feel safe, I wouldn't contact a person no matter what. If I felt like that person was still violent, I wouldn't deal with him or her at all. That's just me. I hope you do not misinterpret my words. This is very important.

Let go of the idea
that you're scared
to open up. Life
transforms when
you choose to
be brave, to be
vulnerable.

—s. mcnutt

If you want to change
your life focus on
being brave. To be
brave means that
you're scared, that
you're the underdog,
but you're still going
to give it everything
you have.

—s. mcnutt□

Stop negotiating
with toxic people.
Run away from
their energy and
save yourself.

—s. mcnutt

You have to cut off
toxic energy as soon
as it starts. If you
don't it will get
deeper and stronger
and will feel normal.
Cut it off.

—s. mcnutt☐

Stop negotiating
with toxic people.
They make you
feel crazy for
being human.

—s. mcnutt☐

Put your happiness
over everything. This
is your life, so don't
worry about what
they will say.

—s. mcnutt☐

A lot of people go wrong
when chaos happens in
their lives because they're
rigid. They obsess about
going backward, forcing
what is broken, and it
never works.

Instead, embrace the
chaos. Believe in staying
fluid and adaptable.
Never try to change what
is happening. Accept
reality, and use your skills
to adapt to it all.

—s. mcnutt

To let go of the past, stop
obsessing about trying to
change what happened.
Healing occurs when you
accept it for what it is.

—s. mcnutt☐

Stop Doing This

Some people never move
on from an ex because
they keep having that
*maybe-sex-will-bring-us-
back-together* sex.

—s. mcnutt

You will never move
on from an ex if you
keep opening up to
him or her. Stop it.
Close the door. Delete
the number. Block the
contact.

—s. mcnutt□

You'll never move
on from someone
if you keep investing
in him or her when
history has proven
that there is no return
on that investment.

—s. mcnutt ☐

You swear up and
down that your ex
is the worst human
being around;
however, you keep
going back.

—s. mcnutt ☐

Walking Away from Toxic

You stop making excuses for the way they treat you. You realize that their manipulation and games will no longer work. You become brave enough to walk away and wise enough to stay away.

—s. mcnutt☐

I genuinely hope you get the happiness you deserve. I hope you have the courage to leave a toxic situation, the strength to recover from one, and the wisdom to know how to avoid them entirely.

—s. mcnutt☐

If you are trying to
leave a toxic situation
and a person tries to
persuade you to stay,
fuck them. They need
to be cut off too.

—s. mcnutt

Let go of the
idea that you
need to
tolerate shitty
behavior.

—s. mcnutt□

Letting go means
allowing your flesh
to shed, your tears
to run, and your heart
to ache. Not forever,
just long enough to
wash all the energy
off you that no longer
deserves to
be there.

—s. mcnutt

Let go of the
need to be right,
the need to prove
a point, and the need
to prove the truth.

—s. mcnutt☐

Closure is not going
back to the toxic
environment that
made you sick.
Closure is staying
away from it,
regardless of how
bad it keeps trying
to bring you back.

—s. mcnutt□

If they made you
sick, they cannot
heal you.

—s. mcnutt

And sometimes it's
not people that we
need to let go of,
because it's not them;
it's us. Sometimes we
have behaviors or
mind-sets that we
have to let go of in
order for the ones
whom we love to stay
around us.

—s. mcnutt

If you have to end
a connection so you
can find happiness
again, do it.

—s. mcnutt□

Let go of the
mind-set that you
never need to leave
your neighborhood,
your state, your little
narrow box.

Growth happens when
you wander into new
spaces.

—s. mcnutt□

Everything changes.
Everyone dies, and
we all take losses.
Get ahead of the
curve and adapt to
change or watch it
destroy you.

—s. mcnutt

Stay away from
people who think they
know everything.
Strive to be the type
of person who knows
that he or she does not
know enough.

—s. mcnutt □

Healing today is
being patient as
you work through
emotional clutter
from yesterday.

—s. mcnutt

Make your life
simpler by reducing
how many decisions
you make each day.

—s. mcnutt□

We hurt ourselves
because we obsess
about the end of our
journeys. Focus on
staying in the
moment, on being
grateful for where
you are today.

—s. mcnutt

Thoughts are seeds;
actions are nutrients.
What type of garden
are you planting?

—s. mcnutt□

In life, the only
two things you
can control are
your effort and
and your attitude.
Everything else
is not up to you.

—s. mcnutt□

FOUR

PEOPLE PLEASING AND SETTING BOUNDARIES

Year after year I used to let people take and take, and I would give and give, and finally I said no. This is my testimony.☐

Changing the Narrative
Around Setting Healthy Boundaries

As children, we do not hear stories about how we should set boundaries between us and other people. The only thing that I remotely remember was "Don't talk to strangers, because strangers are bad." I can see why parents didn't want us to talk to strangers—fear of being kidnapped, fear of an adult overpowering us.

Well, that is actually a flawed mentality. Without talking to strangers, how do we socialize? How do we make friends? How do we find lovers? How do we network and get jobs? "Mom and Dad, if we are not supposed to talk to strangers, how did you two meet to make us?" I said, confused, to my parents. They just looked at me with the *"Boy, stop asking questions and just roll with life"* face when I was a young kid with a million and one questions.

We are conditioned to keep people away from us. When people walk up to us and introduce themselves because they want a date or find us attractive, typically, we say no. We can be lonely as hell, wanting a date and companionship, and we'll flat out lie to these strangers who are being vulnerable because we are conditioned to keep people away from us. We will tell them that we have a boyfriend or girlfriend, knowing that we're lying, when the only thing we have is a liter of wine and a desire to develop partnerships, but we don't, because we are trained to say no to love, to opportunity, to anything that changes our little routines.

The polar opposite of the scenario above is when we completely open up and let people in, but they have shifty morals and crooked intentions—the ones who denigrate us for being human. So here's the real question: Why are we conditioned to keep away strangers? Is it because we fear that they may be bad but reserve spots for people in our lives who have proven their unfavorable positions?

Is it classical conditioning that keeps us running back to people who may not be good for us? Is it our inherent sense of family or loyalty that makes us stay committed to people who are truly toxic? Do you follow where I am going here? Doesn't it seem hypocritical that we are so fearful and weary of *strangers*, but we are welcoming of all the *people we know* even if their actions are egregious, abusive, and malicious?

I believe we have to find some balance with this mind-set. There are some strangers who for sure need to be let into our lives. Sometimes our soul mate is sitting right across from us at the coffee shop, and we never stop to say hello. So it seems that we have to find balance by being willing to allow strangers into our little bubbles. No, not everyone, and not whenever the hell they want, but more often than we are accustomed to. And the other side of that balance is taking these people that we know—whom we love, whom we break bread with, who drive us insane—and figuring out how to implement barriers, boundaries, and a code of conduct for how we will and will not be treated. If you struggle with setting boundaries, this section will shine light on the elements of the practice that I feel are necessary to live an effective and happy life, a life that allows you to remain open to new friends and strangers but also doesn't allow you to get used and abused by familiar faces. But first, let me start off with a story.

This Is Why You
Have to Set Boundaries

I received a phone call one day, and on the other end someone was asking me for almost $2,000 to help cover his monthly finances. I looked at my phone like it was an April Fool's joke. I couldn't believe what I was hearing—a grown adult asking me to cover monthly expenses for him while he sat in his air-conditioned apartment with cable, Wi-Fi, and a 2018 car sitting in the driveway. As my mother used to always say, "Excuse me, but you have me fucked up." What he had asked me for was unreasonable. Two thousand dollars is a month of my living expenses: rent, gas, food, etc. I didn't feel comfortable giving away a month of my savings, and to be clear, I was offended that this was the question.

This was after another person asked me for $600 to help his financial shortcomings; again, this was another adult. That was right after someone else asked me for $950 to help him with a down payment on something he could afford, also another adult. I had to ask myself, after having this very intense ten-to-twelve-day period, "Why the hell do people keep asking me for these big sums of money like I'm the Monopoly Man?" I'm an entrepreneur, a writer. I work hard for my money. It's 4:11 a.m., and I'm up writing about a subject I'm passionate about. I don't understand why they're not up grinding like I am. I work hard for myself, for my brand, and if I get a part-time job again, I will work hard for that company. I am not trying to imply that others are not working hard. I am not saying that I am better than anyone or that anyone else is less than me. I am saying that I choose to live a less fancy life than some people. I choose not to buy fancy clothes. I choose not to get animals, because I cannot afford them. I choose not to get a car note, because I cannot afford it. I am a minimalist who owns ten pairs of jeans and about fifteen shirts. I don't have cable. I don't pay monthly subscriptions for magazines, and now I get my hair done at home. I can't afford the barbershop or salon. I don't buy Starbucks. I cannot afford it, so I get the K-cups from Safeway. I have a monthly budget, and giving money to people who live above their means, who don't use a budget and will simply be asking for it again, is no longer a part of my plan for success. I have to say no. I have to *set boundaries*. I cannot *people please*. I do not feel *guilt* for saying no either (Chapter titles of *Care Package*. Did you catch that?).

Plus, there is another side of this. I remember when I needed to borrow $1,000 from friends. When I got on the phone with my friends when I needed money, I had a plan. I had dates, and I had proof that I would pay them back in less than six weeks. I needed $1,000, so I asked two friends for $500 each. I told them about the new job that I was offered and how it was sixty miles from my residence. They both understood that I needed a new vehicle to ensure that I could make it to this new career. I was living within my means and wasn't asking for money because I was living bigger than my income. My salary was going from about $300–$400 a week as a server and chef to a salary of $28,000 plus commission as a salesperson.

Part of the reason I turned them down is because they didn't have a plan, a way to ensure that my money would come back. Part of the reason I was comfortable asking for money when I needed it was because I had a plan. I had an opportunity for new income, and I knew I wasn't going to go buy things I didn't need. It was 100 percent a need. The second time I needed money was when my father died, and I needed $380 to buy a plane ticket. My cousins put the money together, and I paid them back within a month. I am not into owing people. I am not into people having the upper hand on me. When I die nobody will say that I owe them, but everyone can say that I gave something to them or that I did something for them. This is a conscious choice.☐

Phrases to Say to Help You Set Boundaries

"To be completely honest, that is my personal business, and it is none of your business."

"This is not a threat. I'm just communicating. If you continue to treat me in this way, _____, then I will have to do _____ to protect myself."

"No, I cannot allow you to treat me like this. I do not deserve this. I can't stand for it."

"The last time was the last time that I'll ever be a part of something like that. We do not treat each other like that."

"I've never talked to you with that tone or with those words. We don't talk to each other like that. You cannot speak to me that way."

"What you're asking me to do is simply outside of what I feel comfortable with." ☐

Six Tips on How to Stop
People Pleasing Right Now

1. The very first step is to realize, accept, and understand that this behavior is actually hurting you no matter how much you think you are helping another person.

2. Realize, accept, and understand that this behavior is enabling other people's negative ways instead of encouraging them to grow.

3. Tell yourself that you don't want to feel drained or used any longer.

4. Tell yourself that it is possible to find people who appreciate you—people who do not make you go against yourself.

5. Ask yourself this and answer honestly: If I tell them no, will they be okay? If I tell them yes, even though I want to say no, will I be okay?

6. People pleasing only stops once you stop it. Why would they purposely tell you to stop giving them the benefits that you're willing to provide? The power has always been with you to say no, and once you do, your life will change.

Four Incredible Tips on How to Set Boundaries

1. You have to know what you want, how you want to be treated, or what you deserve to get out of a situation. You'll never stick up for yourself if you don't know why you're doing it in the first place, so know what you want.

2. Communicate that you have been violated, used, or abused. Be very direct, and do not try to spare feelings. It is important that the seriousness of this violation is understood. Be tactful in your execution of explaining this. Communicate with love, and watch your tone.

3. Make suggestions for how a person should treat you. Give them a real-life example of what is okay and what is not, real or hypothetical.

They always say treat people how you want to be treated, but it's deeper than that. Show people how you will or will not be treated by having the power and will to walk away the second it turns abusive, violent, aggressive, or anything that is outside of your boundaries. □

Three Principles on Setting Boundaries That Matter Today

1. Nobody is going to meet you in a place that you haven't met yourself. Nobody is going to all of a sudden say, "Hey, let me respect you when you don't respect you." You must always meet yourself at the level of consciousness that you want other people to meet you at.

2. Assess your boundaries often. You may have set them, but things change, people change, and situations change. It may be time for you to adjust and adapt to a new set of rules for yourself.

3. Remain open-minded, and stay open to change because a boundary doesn't mean forever. A boundary that you set doesn't mean everyone has to follow or by abide by it. Sometimes your boundary can be unfair and can put too much pressure on people, so always check yourself as you set them.

Set Boundaries

You show others how
to treat you based on
how you allow
yourself to be treated.

—s. mcnutt□

Set Boundaries

People respect you
more if you stand up
for yourself, if you
have a backbone.

—s. mcnutt□

Set Boundaries

Walking away
from a toxic
situation is a
form of setting
a boundary.

It's your way
of saying,
"I will not settle
for a poisonous
situation."

—s. mcnutt

To vibrate higher,
we have to be okay
with being alone,
with being patient
while we attract
the right energy.

—s. mcnutt□

Self-love is about
participating in healthy
environments that grow
you and nourish you.
It is also about cutting
yourself off from evil
and energy-draining
environments that kill
you slowly.

—s. mcnutt☐

Nobody will tell you to set
boundaries. All the people
around you benefit from
your giving nature. Check
yourself and slow down if
you're giving too much.

—s. mcnutt☐

You push people
up because your
heart is strong.
Be careful pulling
the ones who pull
you down.

—s. mcnutt□

Set Boundaries

When people treat
you like you're
garbage, look them
right in the eye and
say, *"I am not the
one,"* and then
walk away.

—s. mcnutt□

Set boundaries today,
and your heart will
thank you tomorrow.

—s. mcnutt□

Set Boundaries

Be intentional about
setting a standard for
how you will and will
not be treated.

Set your boundaries
and stick to them so
others know how to
treat you.

—s. mcnutt□

I was eighteen years old. My father
kicked me out of the house, rather
violently, and I had nowhere to go.
My resources were short, and my experience
wasn't long. I sat there with a bag of my
stuff and some four-year-old gym shoes,
and I asked myself, "*What am I going to
do now?*" It was in that moment of
weakness that I became my strongest.
I told myself that I would work for what I
want, that I would become a boss, that I
wouldn't allow anyone to have that
much control over me ever again. It
taught me that crying isn't going to help,
and creating abundance, financially and
spiritually, was my only option.

—s. mcnutt□

When I depended on other
people for shelter, food, clothing,
and permission, I was always at
their mercy. I had to live in their
house and abide by their rules,
physically and emotionally, and
that's not a mental prison that I
deserved to live in. I bossed up.
I put myself first so I could live
freely without feeling trapped or
chained. I set a boundary with
myself: I wouldn't allow any
human to control me like they
were God.

—s. mcnutt

When you have a near-death
experience, all you think
about is life. All you want is
more time and opportunity so
you can live right. Some of
the people in your life are
near-death experiences.
Allow them to teach you
that you need to live your life
more and stress, worry, and
waste time less.

—s. mcnutt☐

If you take the trash
out of the kitchen
and leave it by the
door, what happens?

Your entire house
stinks. Don't cut off
toxic energy halfway.
If you're going to get
rid of it, get rid of it
fully.

—s. mcnutt

Never take it
personally if I
need time to myself.
I don't always
know how to
communicate that
I want to be alone.
People are so
offended these days.

—s. mcnutt□

The hardest people to set boundaries with are family members. Most passionate people are raised to think that you have to always be there for family members because that's what *real love is about*. Sometimes making people be there for themselves is more important than you being there for them. We have to ask ourselves: Am I really helping them, or am I enabling them to keep doing wrong and harm? It's hard to say no to them, but at times it's very necessary.

—s. mcnutt

As you get older, you cannot settle for things you used to settle for. Connections change because what you require out of your interactions changes.

Explaining this to someone from your past is not always easy, because it's hard for people to see growth in others.

Don't guilt yourself if you have to end a connection because they're not respecting your growth.

Maybe they'll come back around when they're ready to vibrate at your level, or maybe they won't.

—s. mcnutt

I hurt myself by
breaking my back for
others, by giving and
giving when nothing
was coming back.

I've decided that the
people who used to
use me have to be cut
off or understand that
I've changed.

The old me died
yesterday, and I have
gone through a rebirth
today. Don't say you
know me until you get
to know the new me.
As of today, you just
knew me.

—s. mcnutt☐

Be More Selfish

If you're a giver, always looking out for others, always feeling drained because you break yourself so others can stay together, take a break from it. Add value to your own life first. Add self-love and peace to your life first.

—s. mcnutt☐

People pleasing is an ugly trait. How can they respect you if you don't respect yourself? How can they grow with you if all you do is break yourself for other people?

—s. mcnutt☐

A Letter on People Pleasing

First off, pat yourself on the back
because you're the type of person who
will continue to give and give to people
around you, and there's no shame in that.
Secondly, you have finally realized that
not everyone deserves the blessing of
your presence—of your giving—and that
is perfectly okay too. You've grown so
much. You require more of people, but at
the core of who you are, you still want to
give first, and that makes you beautiful.
Find people who appreciate you, who
can meet you with your giving and smile
at all the lives you impact.

—s. mcnutt□

On Setting Boundaries

Finally, you have learned and accepted that nobody will ever tell you to take care of you first. Most people care about themselves and their experience, so how can they tell you to take care of you and your experience? We are all living for ourselves until we make beautiful children or until we find a lover who feels like the summertime. And even with them, you still have to learn how to say no, how to change relationships when people take advantage of you, and how to have a backbone when it matters. The world is a tough place if and only if you do not stand up for yourself, and even when you do, others may still find ways to try to pull you down. And what you have to always remember is that what other people do is not up to you. You cannot control it, and you need to simply concern yourself with you and your behavior. Set the boundaries that you need to set and trust the process. It will work out in your favor.

—s. mcnutt

☐

FIVE

GUILT

The definition of guilt: *a feeling of deserving blame for offenses*.

Vulnerable Story on Guilt

Way back in the day, I used to work in the nightclub industry. Yes, pre-social-media boom I was one of the best marketers out there. I was twenty-one years old, the age when most people hit the clubs. I loved the experience because it taught me to value genuine connections. Yes, you can meet good people there, but for the most part everything in that industry is fake; it's all a facade. Of course, you learn this with time, with experience, with alertness, but I didn't know this at first.

I worked there because like any other person fresh out of college, I was in debt, broke, and just trying to get a footing in the world. That's all I was trying to do—network, grow, connect, and get paid. I had many friends who would go with me—friends who worked in the industry and people who would link up every so often, but they weren't friends.

One of my close friends made many poor decisions with me when we were young. Many nights were spent nursing each other because of too much alcohol, and many mornings were spent eating tacos and nachos at five o'clock.

In Chicago there was this spot named Taco Burrito King, and I should be part owner for all the times I've invested in their company as a drunk twentysomething. I like to refer to these episodes as the "I'm broke financially but rich in experience" period of our lives, also known as the "I'm young, so I'm going to do stupid stuff" time.

Of course, you would love to see people in their early twenties secure careers and find themselves, but I am grateful I had a little stupid fun when I was younger. I feel like we are so controlled and limited that we never get to know ourselves until we are in our twenties. College, high school, and living with your parents are all very restrictive, controlled, and for the most part, limiting and confining. How are people supposed to find themselves when they've never been alone, never been allowed to fail, and never learned from people outside their bloodline? Point being, this sacred time put me in the nightclubs after college, talking to women who acted like they were too good for anyone and trying to outdo the next guy who didn't have any money either—the irony. Part of the reason I worked at the clubs was so I did not have to pay to get in—duh. But what do you think happened? What always happens: *it got old*. I outgrew it. I got tired of dealing with energy that didn't vibrate with me, and I removed myself from that environment.

When I moved on, I really moved on. I stopped

drinking. I stopped partying. I stayed off the scene. No bars. No clubs. No girls. Nothing. Just me and my solitude. Me and my new job that I loved. I was fortunate enough to put myself in a situation where I had a salary and commission in my new sales career away from the city, tucked away in a little suburb called Wheaton, Illinois. It was my first "big-boy" job, as they say, and I didn't want to blow it because I was out partying too much. Time out: to be truthful and transparent here, I still went once I got the job, just not as much.

As I settled into this new job, I slowly faded out of the scene. One day I was all work and no play, which was fine, because I was all play and no work at one point. As I grew and matured, my friends didn't advance at my pace, and as you grow, you will experience the exact same thing. When you see that you've outgrown situations, friends, and behaviors that now seem toxic, you look at them with a strange eye when everyone else thinks they're normal. That is how you know that you are going through a spiritual awakening.

How the Guilt Started
during My Spiritual Awakening

As I started to fade away from the scene, the

people who needed me to go to the clubs kept calling. The ones who benefited from my extroversion called and texted. The women who wanted to use my power for free drinks, discounted bottles, or attention at the hottest clubs kept calling. The guys who wanted to use me because there was always a pretty girl or group of them around me kept calling, and what do you think happened?

I went back. Not because I wanted to but because like you, I didn't understand that I was a people pleaser. Even though some of these connections were weak and fleeting, fake and disingenuous; even though these environments caused me pain, didn't bring me joy, and left me drained, I still went because I wanted to please other people. Once you feel that type of inner guilt, that is the exact moment you have to take control of your life.

When you're young, you may not get this. You may act young, silly, goofy, and you might not take life seriously, which is fine. Be carefree, but the moment you realize that you're outgrowing things, be ready to distance yourself from friends; otherwise they will suck you back in. You're going to say yes because you don't take yourself seriously enough, and truthfully, you may not be just a young person who has this issue. You can be in your fifties and still have this struggle. I just had a book reading in Phoenix, and most of the people there were in their late twenties to midthirties. Even people in the middle of their lives have trouble saying no to friends, family, and coworkers.

You have the boss who always asks you to stay late. Even though you can't, you stay anyway. You stay because you haven't read what we talked about in the last chapter: saying no and setting boundaries.

In my situation, I tried my best to distance myself, to stay away, but I never set boundaries. I never said no because it was what I meant. I was only able to say no once another person would feel my guilt and let me off the hook. I don't want you to wait until other people let you off the hook. I want you to learn this now.

You will outgrow people. It will confuse them, and when this happens you have to realize that the friendship may truly be over. Do not allow people from your past to guilt you into what you used to do and who you used to be if those behaviors cause you pain. You don't have to go back to being the person who you want to be just because your old friends want you to return there. You can say no, you can turn them down, and you can ascend to new heights without going back to your old ways. If you are struggling with ascending, feeling like you're not being a good friend or partner, it's probably because you're dealing with an inner dialogue that isn't helpful.

How to Deal with Inner Guilt

1. Realize and accept that you do not have to own the guilt. It's not your responsibility.
2. You feel guilt because you outgrew people, but that's a normal process that occurs in life, and you should look at growth as a positive experience, not a negative one.
3. It's not your responsibility to ensure that other people grow, especially other adults, because we are all in charge of ourselves.
4. Realize that acting like a superhero will always hurt you. Help people when you can. Show up when you can, but you're not obligated to do everything or be everywhere for everyone else all the time.
5. Life has always been and will always be the survival of the fittest. Those who grow, who adapt, who get stronger and wiser, and who adjust their behavior are the ones who will live happily. If other human beings consciously choose not to evolve, don't feel like it's your fault they didn't or your responsibility to make them. □

Phrases to Help Communicate Guilt as You Feel It So You Can Let It Go in That Moment

"If I could help you, I would. But at this moment, I am unable to."

"I'm sorry to hear what you're going through. What actions have you taken to fix/solve this?"

"I want to understand where you're coming from right now. Are you venting to me, or are you asking me for help?"

"I know pride might be killing you, but if you need help, you must communicate it directly to me. I do not understand the indirect gestures."

"I am not in a position to help."

"I do not have the ability to help."

"I know for a fact that you'll get through this situation. If I could do more, I would. But I am unable to fulfill that request.☐

You will outgrow
people. It will
confuse them.
No matter what,
stay on your path.

—s. mcnutt

Everyone has to save
themselves from their
own messes.

—s. mcnutt□

Don't say anything
negative about
yourself because
others do. Another
person's opinion of
you is not a fact.

—s. mcnutt

Remember this:
everyone else is
scared, everyone else
doesn't know who
they are, and most
people give up on
their dreams. Don't
listen to them.

—s. mcnutt □

Empaths Who Give Too Much

You have such a big heart that it causes
you to get in your own way sometimes.
You lend a helping hand before people ask
you for it. You feel guilt and discomfort
when you're unable to help. You go out
of your way all the time when others
don't go out of their way for you or even
themselves. You give like it's your job.
You support friends. You are a good
person, but if you're feeling guilty
because you can't be there, it's okay.
You have spent your entire life being
in everyone's corner, and you've reached
that point in your life where you need to
be there for yourself. Save yourself this time.

—s. mcnutt

A Letter on Guilt

When I was younger, I was given phrases and teachings like everyone else: Don't be too loud. Be nice to people. Be kind. Always help people out if you can, especially family. And now that I am older, I don't believe in any of that blindly. I help if I can help. I risk my life, my resources, or what I have going on only when I am able to. I will not break myself, my bank account, my mental health, or my peace of mind just because I need to save someone. I believe in people learning from their mistakes like I did. I want to help. By nature I am giving, but I am no longer married to the guilt that comes with saying no. I have divorced the guilt that comes from walking away from commitments that used to be great but have since turned poor. Now I live by this: save yourself. That doesn't mean that I am heartless, don't care, or will not help. It simply means that I do care, but I have to always check and double-check before I risk breaking my inner peace.

—s. mcnutt☐

How You Know You're Going Through a Spiritual Awakening

It feels like you've outgrown
situations, friends, and behaviors
that were once normal because
now they seem toxic to you.
What society has accepted as
normal is actually strange to you.
You stop caring about fitting in.
You accept that you were born to
stand out, to build your own path.

—s. mcnutt☐

Toxic environments do
not create healthy people.
You may have overcome
the worst, but to reach
your best, you have to
heal from the pain those
toxic environments
created.

—s. mcnutt☐

You can say no, you can
turn them down, and you
can ascend to new heights
without going back to
your old ways. If they
don't like it, let them deal
with their inner conflicts.

—s. mcnutt□

Stand your ground.
If you're not
comfortable with
the situation, say no.
Life goes on.

—s. mcnutt□

Don't give fourth and fifth
chances for people to keep
hurting you like they did the
first, second, and third time.
Be forgiving but not stupid.
These aren't mistakes. This
is true behavior. Don't feel
guilty for walking away
from destructive behavior.

—s. mcnutt

If you look back
objectively and feel
like you did everything
you could, then you do
not deserve to allow the
guilt to eat you alive today.

—s. mcnutt □

Making Guilt Lighter So
You Can Get Rid of It!

We aren't done talking about guilt. This is one of the most important subjects I'll ever write about. After writing this entire book, I realized I was holding on to a massive amount of guilt, and holding on to guilt was stopping me from moving forward. *Care Package* helped me greatly. I hope you're getting value out of these vulnerable stories, poems, and quotes.

Who will run faster: you at five hundred pounds or you at two hundred pounds? Of course the smaller version will move faster because the mass is much smaller. Think of guilt like an extra three hundred pounds.

It's dangerous to your life, and it's dangerous to your progress. In fact, it keeps you on a constant plateau. It keeps you in a state of fear, a state of anxiety.

Understanding how guilt works will help you understand codependency. It will help you understand why you don't set boundaries. It will help you understand how to love yourself deeper. These topics are all intertwined, and that is why *Care Package* is the most important book I've written.

In *Lust For Life*, I talked about developing

abundance. I talked about getting on a budget and saving money. I talked about building your business or getting promoted at the job. In *Lust For Life*, I talked about how you deserve to experience life and to be rich in experience, but there is another element that comes with that, which is something I am truly experiencing now that is rooted in guilt. Right now I want to talk to you about survivor's guilt and how unbundling guilt will help you reach more abundance in life.

Survivor's Guilt

A modern-day example of survivor's guilt occurred in the movie *The Hunger Games*. If you observe Katniss, the protagonist, you can see that she suffers immensely with survivor's guilt. She is haunted and corrupted by the deaths she causes and the deaths she is around through the Hunger Games elimination competitions.

The universe is always in alignment, and I literally just watched all four movies this past weekend for the first time. It's ironic to me that while I am writing about guilt, I observe a protagonist who suffers greatly from survivor's guilt—a protagonist who helped me understand myself and my life deeper. *The Hunger Games* is like *The Matrix* trilogy, a movie series that has deeper analogies related to our society, to how we are conditioned, and to how we treat one another. These films use entertainment to make us think about ourselves.

Survivor's guilt is an experience a person feels when he or she survives something traumatic. I can flat-out tell you that this is something I have dealt with my entire life. I am from Chicago, and all we know is struggle. Being a black man in a country that still doesn't like black men is traumatic. Every day I have to walk around and make sure I'm less threatening or prove to people that I am no danger to them, because the media loves to paint distorted images of black men. When you look back in time, you'll see the new movie *Black Panther* is one of the greatest movies of all time, and it's mostly an all-black cast that broke the stereotypical roles given to black actors. I don't have the platform that Hollywood has, but one of my underlying goals with my social media, with my brand, and with my books is to control my narrative, to show you that we destroy stereotypes where I come from.

I was involved in a school shooting where six people were killed (NIU, Valentine's Day 2008.) I've watched my friends be abused by their parents, and we thought it was normal. The first three girlfriends I had were all raped or sexually abused when they were younger, and so I grew up thinking that all women went through sexual abuse.

Think about a slave who is born into slavery. They'll have a hard time desiring freedom because they may not know that it is even possible. I was conditioned to all this stuff, and it made me cold. It made me savage, and it made me not trust anyone from my environment.

Being from Chicago, it's everyone against everyone. There is no love. It felt like I was in a war outside of the house, dealing with racism, mean girls, and teachers who never let me express myself when I was a child. Combine all that with what I had to go through at home: two abusive parents who were verbally abusive, physically coercive, and emotionally absent. I lived through hell already, in my opinion.

Both parents being emotional unavailable was one of the key components that led me down the path of being a writer. There was no one for me to have an open-ended conversation with. Everything in my household was manipulated, judged, or controlled. There was no freedom to simply be who you are. As a result, they created an angry child who felt like he had to survive—a child who felt like he had no friends, couldn't trust anyone, and if he didn't save himself, then nobody would be there for him. This is what I dealt with, and it's who I was.

I had the me-against-the-world mind-set—survivor's mind-set, warrior mind-set. People who have come from similar backgrounds are often the hardest workers because we try to create a new identity through our work. We are often great at sports or music because we always have constant inspiration to draw from. People like me are often closed off and unwilling to open up, something *Care Package* is helping us do.

Look back on the profile I described. I am certainly not that person today. I am not those stories today. I am simply shining a light on a level of consciousness that I once had to help you see the contrast between what happened to me and to what is happening to me so we can dissect what survivor's guilt truly is.

One of the reasons why you read my work, in my little opinion, is because I've been through hell and survived. I've been through so much pain, and yet my message is love. My message is healing. My message is that we can overcome, and that inspiration is what everyone needs in their lives. I believe that is the reason why you have found me among others.

Today I am happy. I have forgiven. I have made peace with so much and moved forward. I have been able to help millions of people do the same thing.

To me, I feel rich. I don't know what other people consider rich, but I feel rich. I have no debt. I own my car. I have money in my emergency fund. I have investments. I am intentional to keep my income high and my expenses low. I am focused on living as simply as possible and not buying excessive things that I don't need. I am not into consumerism. I am into living below means and remaining grateful for what you have.

I have healthy relationships and friendships. I have healthy habits, with my yoga and weight lifting practices. I am mindful and minimal with my possessions. I have a job I like and a life I love. I get a lot of fulfillment out of the life that I live. I have found my passion, which is to be vulnerable and to use my talent to inspire people. I have found my passion, which is to take care of my health and to have fun. I have found my passion, which is to invest time and energy into relationships, to travel, and to eat new foods often.

And this is where survivor's guilt creeps in. You say to yourself, "Damn, why did I make it through, and they didn't?" You end up asking yourself why you were luckier or more fortunate than the others who died when they were put in the same situation as you.

You look at your brother and sister and friends and family and wish they could feel what you feel or that they could be blessed the way you are, and that is when the guilt comes all over your body. You want to travel, to live, to smile, and you see people you're close to in depression, broke, and run-down. So you ask yourself why you were chosen to win. To answer that question, you have found *Care Package*.

Do a job you like.
Build a life you love.
—s. mcnutt

You can find a lot of
value and purpose
within the work you
do. Show up on time,
put value into your
work, and always be
willing to learn.

—s. mcnutt☐

One of the keys of
power is to always
control the narrative:
don't let others tell
your side of the story.

—s. mcnutt□

How are people
supposed to find
themselves when
they've never been
alone, never been
allowed to fail?

—s. mcnutt

Life is a mix of victories
and defeats. Appreciate
the victories and learn
from the defeats. Stay
humble through all the
winning and never
turn against yourself
when you take losses.

—s. mcnutt□

Note To Self:

You are only responsible
for your own experience.
Save yourself. Be the
hero you need for you
today, tomorrow, and
everyday thereafter.

—s. mcnutt□

Never stay in a relationship
only because you're afraid
you will hurt them more by
breaking up. That is the
wrong reason to stay
together. You're hurting
yourself more and more each
day. They are responsible for
their feelings and healing
process, not you.

—s. mcnutt☐

Learning to
not guilt-trip
yourself might
be hard, but it is
not impossible.

—s. mcnutt☐

We feel guilt when we say no
because we are used to feeling like
we are obligated to be a superhero,
and we feel obligated to save people
from their own problems. Saying no
does not make you a villain. In fact,
if you want to survive this life, you'll
have to be your own hero and
practice the art of saving yourself.

—s. mcnutt

All you can do is be yourself,
present the most organic
version of yourself and allow
the rest to play itself out.
You are not responsible for
what people do or do not
understand.
—s. mcnutt☐

SIX

CODEPENDENCY

I was codependent.
I was codependent.
I was codependent.

This is how I broke
out of it and why
you could too. □

☐   I came from a dysfunctional home, a home that had two alcoholics, a home that shut down feelings and tough conversations. That kind of energy produces a deep level of codependency.

Many people have codependent behaviors, and they never realize it. Understanding codependency and taking action to prevent it not only manifests healthy relationships but can also help you leave toxic ones.

Being able to identify codependency can stop you from jumping into cycles of pain, cycles of mistrust, and cycles of pure dysfunction. In *Codependent No More*, Melody Beattie loosely gives these words as a way to identify codependency: if concern has turned into obsession; if compassion has turned into caretaking; or if you are taking care of other people and not taking care of yourself, you may be struggling with codependency. Each person must decide for him- or herself if codependency is a problem. Each person must decide for him- or herself what needs to be changed and when that should happen. People who grow up with alcoholics, are friends with people who have eating disorders, or who are friends with severely insecure people often fall into codependency. They fall into the trap of trying to save someone, even if it means they lose themselves in the process. The term is vague because it's truly up to people to determine for themselves if they are indeed codependent, and once they do, then and only then can they adjust behavior. Beattie goes on to say, "As far as an origin of the word goes, professionals had long suspected something peculiar happened to people who were closely involved with chemically dependent people."

Personally, I grew up with two alcoholic parents, and as a result, I became an adult who often thought he needed to save people, who needed to care about people's results more than they do. And if I was not *helping* people, then I was not fulfilled, because it felt like it was my duty to help. That is the inner dialogue of codependency. After being objective and honest with myself and doing a lot of reflecting, I saw that I needed to break up with those mind-sets. Like you, I thought to myself, *"Well, people are going to think I don't care and that I am some savage if I am not jumping in helping them."* Here's what I realized: it doesn't matter what people think about you. What matters is what you think about you. It's hard to come to that agreement with yourself at first because codependency has taught us that saving the world is just more important than saving ourselves, and it's not. In fact, you will save the world if you save yourself. You will change the world if you change yourself. And that's the part that we do not get when we are blindly following codependent behaviors. Once I elevated myself, made barriers and boundaries, my friendships and connections changed. I met new people who cared about valuing me and cherishing me. The old people who had been there when I was Superman stepped up to the challenge of meeting my new energy.

Some people faded away because they simply couldn't vibrate at this new level, but that is okay. Everyone cannot stay around once you elevate. I'm willing to bet my next cup of water that if you elevated yourself, you would have the same effect. You would make people treat you better simply because you treated yourself better. Freeing yourself from codependency, in my opinion, all starts in your mind, and then gets executed through a change in behavior. In order to change behavior, we have to change mind-set. Changing mind-set is all about seeing the value of the change or adjustment. I cannot tell you why you need to stop being codependent. But for me, I wanted to stop saving people. I wanted to stop hurting myself. I wanted to free myself of guilt. I wanted to look out for me first because nobody else was. I wanted to use my hard-earned resources for my life.□

Activity to Help Attack Codependency

1. Do some independent research on what codependency is to you because your □ definition of it matters too.

2. Write down an action plan. Identify which behaviors you do that you do not like, and create a plan to work on reducing them until you reach the point where you can get rid of them.

3. Use a daily journal to write your experiences. Doing this will allow you to go back and see your stories and experiences and eventually learn from them.□

The number-one thing
I had to stop doing
was trying to jump in
and save people from
their own decisions.
I had to realize that
saving people is
enabling them to do
it again. I was hurting
more than I was helping.
—s. mcnutt☐

Codependency has
taught us that saving
the world is more
important than saving
ourselves, and it's not.
In fact, you will save
the world if you save
yourself.

—s. mcnutt☐

Are you really saving
someone else if you
lose yourself during
the process of helping
them?

—s. mcnutt☐

They may never
speak of the hard
times they're going
through. All they
need is an ear that
will listen, a hug,
and to know someone
cares deeply.

—s. mcnutt☐

Life is survival of
the fittest. If people
are doing things that
are killing them, that
doesn't mean you
have to participate.
Save yourself.

—s. mcnutt□

If you fight for it, I'll
fight with you. If you
don't want to fight for
it, then I have to find
someone who wants
it as bad as I do.

—s. mcnutt

Stop begging people
to call you back, to
respond to your texts,
to like you, to commit
to you, and to be your
friend. That's fake.
—s. mcnutt☐

When the connection
is genuine, you never
have to beg someone
for attention or
respect.
—s. mcnutt☐

Break up with the
behavior of chasing
adults who don't want
to communicate. Life
is too short to waste
precious energy with
them, when there are
adults who love to
communicate.
—s. mcnutt☐

I enjoy being alone.
I'm not lonely when
I'm alone. I'm just in
"my zone." The right
people and energy
will easily bring me
out of my zone. If
they have the wrong
 energy for me, then
I'd rather stay in my
zone.

—s. mcnutt ☐

SEVEN

Self-Care and Putting Yourself First

I just heard a girl list the top-ten things in her life that she cares about most, and she didn't list herself. This is the problem we are dealing with.☐

How you treat
yourself today
is the blueprint
for how others
will treat you
tomorrow.

—s. mcnutt

If you treat yourself well
and there are people who
are committed to treating
you like trash, at some
point you have to
acknowledge that their
behavior isn't about you,
and it's a reflection of
them. Walking away is
your duty at this point.

—s. mcnutt□

Remove yourself from people who treat you like your time doesn't matter, like your feelings are worthless, or like your soul is replaceable.

—s. mcnutt

Healing is Important

We experience trauma directly through our experiences and indirectly by empathizing with friends, the news, and even strangers.

We owe it to ourselves to seek healing—therapy, detoxes, moments of solitude, physical fitness, etc.

—s. mcnutt

Top-Ten Secrets to Implementing True Self-Love Today

1. Caring less about others' opinions.
2. Telling yourself positive affirmations daily, not to create delusion but to create inner support.
3. Understanding that it's okay to be aware of what you dislike about yourself, but that doesn't mean you have to beat yourself up about it.
4. Taking time for yourself every day and being selfish with your energy and time.
5. Telling people no if it's hurting you, breaking you, draining you, or causing unruliness.
6. Saying yes to something new—experiences, opportunities, people, life, ideas, hobbies.
7. Deleting all the sad songs off your playlist and jamming out to new ones—the ones that make you dance, the ones that make you laugh and party.
8. Self-Care Day: spa, haircut, gym, massage, sauna, chiropractor, yoga, nails, hair style.
9. Giving love to others and not expecting it back is also a form of self-love.
10. Celebrating the small victories when you grow, mature, or overcome something.

Do not break
yourself by
trying to keep
someone else
together.

—s. mcnutt

If I have to go out of my way
to keep your life together, to
keep you ticking, to keep you
motivated for your own
goals, then that means you
are my dependent child, and I
will do everything in my
power to help you. If you are
not my child, do not get mad
when I tell you to deal with
your own life. I will not
break myself to keep another
adult together.

—s. mcnutt□

Avoid people who
always have bad
things happen to
them. They are
attracting it more
than they know.

—s. mcnutt

In the long run, the
people who succeed a
little often succeed a
lot. The people who
keep losing in life get
used to losing: proof
that mind-set plus
action is everything.

—s. mcnutt□

This new you knows
how to set boundaries;
this new you knows
how to run away from
energy that is corrupt
and evil.

—s. mcnutt

Embracing Boundaries

I set healthy boundaries
with people now. I am
unwilling to surround
myself with dark energy
just because other people
are okay with it. I am
okay alone. I am okay
with walking far
distances, literally or
figuratively, in order for
me to escape that energy.

—s. mcnutt☐

Don't spend any more time
on unrequited love. Pouring
energy into someone who
doesn't pour it into you only
drains you. There is a person
who will appreciate your love
—one who doesn't want to
drain you, one who wants to
give back. Find that soul.

—s. mcnutt□

Stop pouring your heart
into the heartless.

—s. mcnutt

It's okay to pour
your heart out into
other people;
however, self-love
teaches you that even
the biggest giver still
needs it to come back.

—s. mcnutt☐

It's not selfish to want
love back—it's
human.

—s. mcnutt☐

Nowadays I love
like this: I will give
everything I have
twice, but my lover
has to at least give
me 110 percent of
what they have too.

—s. mcnutt

I live like this: If you
treat me well, I will
treat you better. If you
give me enough, I will
give you more.

—s. mcnutt□

Tell your lover that it's okay to tell you no. Tell your lover that they should not break their back for you if they don't have to. If you truly have a great partner, tell them that your goal is to be a great partner, too, and that you never want them to feel used or overworked.

—s. mcnutt☐

Sometimes you need time alone to do things for yourself that make your life better. This is called self-care and recharging. Take time to add value back into yourself.

—s. mcnutt☐

When you need
self-care time,
communicate it,
and never make
yourself feel
guilty about the
process of taking
care of self.

—s. mcnutt

You love the same way I do
—all in, giving too much,
loving too hard, and never
looking out for yourself,
because you put others first.
I will never tell you to stop;
however, I will tell you to be
patient with dating because
people like us have to pick
the right partner. For us,
the right partner will either
build us or destroy us.

—s. mcnutt☐

I hope you get to
be with someone
who is a home and
an adventure—a soul
who calms you and
drives you wild.

—s. mcnutt

Self-love is picking
the right partner, the
right job, and the right
mind-sets to live with.

—s. mcnutt☐

Words are extremely
powerful. Never use
them to destroy; use
them to build.

—s. mcnutt

We always forget
to thank ourselves
for the progress that
we have made on
our journeys. Imagine
how we would feel if
we didn't focus on
how far we needed to
go, but instead we
focused on how far
we have come.

—s. mcnutt☐

They say you're selfish
for putting yourself first;
however, self-preservation
is a behavior that ensures
an organism's survival.

How are you selfish for
trying to make sure that
you survive?

—s. mcnutt

There is this little voice in our heads
that tells us to be quiet, to care about
everyone else's needs, and to break
our spirits, all in the name of helping
another person. Who the hell is
going to help us? Who is going to
look out for us? Nobody will; it's up
to you to put yourself first. It's up to
you to tell that voice that you need to
put yourself first for a while.

—s. mcnutt☐

It is sexy to me
when you take
care of yourself.
Love you so I
can love you too.

—s. mcnutt

I need time to
myself—space
to grow my mind,
to heal deeply,
to learn who I
really am.

—s. mcnutt☐

Some people don't
understand the importance
of solitude. I don't always
want to be stimulated.
I don't always want noise.
In fact, when I find my
alone time, that's when I
find myself. Alone time
helps me put myself first.
It helps me reset life.

—s. mcnutt

My personality confuses people.
I enjoy being alone, a lot, but
I'm very social and outgoing.
My environment dictates how I
behave. Sometimes I'm loud,
sometimes I'm quiet. I read the
energy and adjust. There are
times when I want to turn up
with others and then there are
moments when I want to read a
good book, or process thoughts,
alone. I am an ambivert.

— s.mcnutt□

I need to be alone from
time to time. Never think
this desire of mine is
because of something you
did or did not do. It's not
personal; I am wired like this.

—s. mcnutt

I no longer have space for
friends or family members
or lovers who do not
understand that I must be
afforded time to myself.
I will communicate it, I
will show it, and I will be
consistent with my efforts
to put care into myself.
I will love you more when
you understand this about me.
I will love you forever when
you allow me to navigate
my alone time.

—s. mcnutt□

In the generation of
cellphones and online
profiles, I still crave
genuine human
connection. I love
sharing positive energy
and laughter with others
more than I love online.

—s. mcnutt

I am in my zone when I am
alone. The right people will
easily bring me out of my
zone because nothing
compares to a genuine
connection. Most people have
the wrong energy, and they
keep me in my zone since I
no longer have time for
ulterior motives and
disingenuous actions.

—s. mcnutt □

Be mindful, extremely selective,
and very intentional about the
people you allow in your life.
Not enough people are talking
about how life-altering this is.

—s. mcnutt

I don't want to be around
pettiness, passive-aggressiveness,
unnecessary anger, extreme
bitterness, or any person who
brings me a nonpeaceful
vibration.

—s. mcnutt☐

I don't want to beg
for communication,
for understanding.
I am comfortable in
my own world, alone
in my own space. If
you want me to
connect with you,
please bring a mature
and peaceful vibe;
otherwise I would
rather be left alone.

—s. mcnutt☐

We crave consistency
so much that it kills
desire. Relationships
need to have desire to
last, to me, it is one of
the most powerful
elements. Spend time
apart so you can miss
each other, so you can
crave connection from
one another.

—s. mcnutt☐

Most people don't
understand how
draining they are.
If you need time
to yourself, take it.

—s. mcnutt

Don't allow people to
make you feel bad
because you enjoy
alone time or time to
yourself to gather
your energy.

There's nothing wrong
with keeping to yourself
and minding
your own business.

—s. mcnutt☐

This culture makes
it seem like you have
to slave away at a
career to be happy.

I don't agree...

—s. mcnutt

There has to be balance
between work, life,
education, friendships, and
relationships. If you do not
find the healthy balance, it is
possible that you will always
suffer. You have limited
energy and limited hours in a
day, so work diligently
toward what's important to
you, and realize that if you
don't know how to balance,
something will always suffer.

—s. mcnutt□

Environment is truly
everything in life. You
can't settle for just
anything. Cultivate a
space that lifts you
and others up and not
one that holds
everyone down.

—s. mcnutt

Sometimes a good
soul will stay with the
wrong person for too
long, and it turns
them bad. You have
permission to walk
away if the situation
is pulling the worst
behaviors out of you.
Nobody is going to
save you. Save
yourself.

—s. mcnutt□

I want to cultivate
environments that
produce ideas,
sunshine, and laughter
for everyone I know.
We have all felt the
depths of darkness
for too long.

—s. mcnutt

I have to create and sustain an
environment that is healthy. It's not
just about me. It's about the kids, my
lover, and my family. We all deserve
to live in consistently healthy spaces.
I will do whatever I have to do to
cultivate this space. I'm putting
myself first because all these people
need me to be at my best.

—s. mcnutt□

Don't stay in a
toxic environment
and expect it to
give you clean air.
If you want to
breathe again,
you know what you
need to do.

—s. mcnutt

You'll feel a million
times better when you
leave that toxic
relationship that you no
longer deserve to be in.
If you haven't had the
strength to leave, just
know, your future self
is begging you to put
yourself first right now.
—s. mcnutt□

When it is time
to go, be gone.
Stop convincing
yourself to stay
in unwanted
environments.

—s. mcnutt

Your own joy comes
first. Eliminate anything
that threatens your
ability to stay happy.
Jobs can go. Fake
friends go. Those bad
habits and terrible
mindsets that slow you
down, must go. Take
control of your life, you
only get one. You are
strong enough to do
this.

—s. mcnutt☐

If the job is toxic, leave.
You can get money from
a career that doesn't ruin
your happiness and health.

—s. mcnutt

Some people
come into your
life to teach
you a lesson.
Not everyone is
permanent.

—s. mcnutt□

Life is one big wave.
Learn how to flow
and understand when
it's time to let go.

— s. mcnutt

Sometimes everything hits
you all at once. You lose a
relationship, change jobs, and
old friends go and new
friends come. It's up one day
and down the next. You have
it all together on Monday,
and by Thursday you don't
have a clue. Life is one big
wave, and all we can do is
flow, grow, and adapt.

— s. mcnutt □

I am not for everyone,
but once you taste my
energy, you'll always
be thirsty.

—s. mcnutt

You can learn something
from everyone but you also
do not have to.Some people
have energy that just doesn't
combine well like oil and water.

—s. mcnutt☐

When your emotions
get the best of you,
pause, breathe, gather
facts, and allow things
to play out. Self-care
is being patient versus
blowing up.

—s. mcnutt☐

Emotional people
make situations worse
because they stop
thinking. They
respond with ego.
Sit back, inhale
deeply, and approach
it methodically.

—s. mcnutt☐

Breakup with the negative
self-talk, with telling yourself
what you cannot do, with
self-sabotage. Get angry about
this and use the anger to power
you. You're worth more than
what you've allowed, and now,
it's time to get serious about
yourself. You can do this.
Save yourself.
—s. mcnutt

Self-love is putting
yourself in as many
situations that allow
you to smile, to hug,
and to feel valued
and wanted.

—s. mcnutt☐

EIGHT

OVERCOMING ANXIETY

The hardest thing a young boy will do in his life is go talk to the pretty girl in his class. He plays the scenario over in his head a million times.

Overthinking may ruin
happiness and opportunity,
and it can create unneeded
anxiety. You're overthinking
so much because you want to
control the outcomes. The
only thing you can control is
your effort and your attitude
—that's it. Alternative: tell
yourself you deserve it and
then take the necessary
actions so you can earn it.

—s. mcnutt

Overthinking is the biggest
waste of human energy.
Trust yourself, make a
decision, and gain more
experience. There is no such
thing as perfect. You cannot
think your way into
perfection, just take action.

—s. mcnutt☐

A lot of us are afraid
to face ourselves, and
that is why we run
from growth, love, or
opportunity. Instead,
we run into anxiety.

— s. mcnutt

What would happen to
your life if you stopped
disliking that thing about
yourself that someone
else told you to dislike?

— s. mcnutt□

Spend less time
overthinking and
more time trusting
your intuition and
setting boundaries.

—s. mcnutt□

If your intuition tells
you that something is
off, pause, don't react
emotionally right
away, and be patient
as you fully observe
behavior and energy.

—s. mcnutt

If you want your
relationship to be
beautiful, you have
to be comfortable
with having
uncomfortable
and sometimes
ugly conversations.

—s. mcnutt☐

When I had the most
anxiety, it was because
I wanted to control
every outcome. I was
not confident in myself
and overthought every
scenario forty-seven
times. Once I broke up
with the need to control
the external, the anxiety
went away.

—s. mcnutt☐

Mindfulness allows
you to stay in the
moment. Staying in
the moment allows
you to not stress or
worry about the
future. This practice
eases and eliminates
anxiety.

—s. mcnutt□

Mindfulness is the
ability to fill your
mind with your full
attention to the present moment.

Mindfulness allows
you to stay here, to
erase anxiety, because
anxiety is created via
stress from a future
event, outcome, or
emotion.

—s. mcnutt□

Never stress about money; the stress only makes it worse than it has to be.

—s. mcnutt

Make a written budget and commit to it. Increase your income and decrease your expenses. Lastly, tell yourself that you are worthy of financial abundance and then trust the process.

—s. mcnutt□

No matter how much
you worry, complain,
or stress out about
something, the result
will still be the same.
Learn to live in a
space of acceptance.
It will free you.

—s. mcnutt□

Your anxiety exists
because you are
uncertain about the
outcome of certain
events, and the truth
is, nothing in life is
certain—nothing.

—s. mcnutt□

Some anxiety is
based on irrational
fears. Ask yourself:
"How real is this fear
in this moment?"

—s. mcnutt

If you don't examine
your fears, they will
control you for the
rest of your life.
Sometimes, you have
to be brave and wild,
and just say, "Fuck it;
I trust myself; let's
see what happens."

—s. mcnutt □

I used to have a bad case
of anxiety with certain
situations and people. It
went away for me when I
realized every human has
a level of an anxiety that
they experience. When I stop
judging myself and when I
learned to trust my intuition,
the anxiety went away and
life became easy for me..

—s. mcnutt

Fear makes your anxiety
spike, and that's why you
have to change the
dialogue in your head
about what real fear is
versus what you have
 created.

—s. mcnutt☐

If you get panic attacks
caused by anxiety,
remember this:

breathe and pause. You
will have thoughts, but
try your best to have
positive inner thoughts
while breathing deeply.

—s. mcnutt□

There is no value
in allowing others'
opinions to rule who
you are or who
you're going to be.

—s. mcnutt□

One of the best
ways to worry less
and smile more is
to remove the
obsessive need to
control outcomes
or perceptions.

*To be okay with
what is.*

—s. mcnutt☐

If you struggle with
anxiety, you have
to applaud yourself
every single time
you step outside of
your comfort zone.

—s. mcnutt☐

We are all guilty of
obsessing about the end
point of the journey, and
the truth is, there is no
end point to any journey.
Everything is connected.
Everything matters, and
this is why you have to
learn to appreciate the
moments, to be totally
immersed in the journey.

—s. mcnutt☐

Dear Human Dealing with Anxiety,

In some cases, your anxiety is normal.
Anxiety itself is an experience that
every person feels on some level.
It's okay and normal to experience
anxiety, nervousness, angst, and worry
throughout life. I've found that the key
to healing social anxiety, self-doubt,
overthinking, and worry. They went
away when I did two things: First,
I started controlling my breathing.
Second, I started to control my inner
dialogue about what I was experiencing.
If this doesn't help, please see a therapist
and please do not have any shame about it.
It's okay if you need help. It's okay if you
want to talk to a professional about it, one
who can help you declutter your experience.

With compassion,

Sylvester McNutt III

NINE

LIVING IN THE MOMENTS

A collection of words, thoughts, and poems that were inspired by the art of staying in the moment.☐

When was the last
time you turned the
phone off, stayed
away from
social media and the
news, and just sat
with yourself?

—s. mcnutt

Stay in the Moment

The practice of
staying present will
heal you. Obsessing
about how the future
will turn out creates
anxiety. Replaying
broken scenarios from
the past causes anger
or sadness. Stay here,
in this moment.

—s. mcnutt☐

Just Handle It

Don't worry or
allow yourself to
stress about problems.
They come. You
apply attention and
energy to them, and
then they go away.

—s. mcnutt

The idea that you
have to "figure out"
your entire life by the
time you're twenty-
five makes me laugh.
Life doesn't work that
way. Stay self-aware,
focus on growth, and
just enjoy every
moment.

—s. mcnutt☐

I am the type of person
who needs to move
forward more than I need
to stay stuck in the past.

—s. mcnutt

I don't derive my
sense of self from
who I was in the
past. I have grown.
I am who I am today.
I live in the present
energy of who I am
today.

—s. mcnutt▢

I have learned to
live in a space of gratitude —
staying grateful for what I
have, learning from what I
have lost,
and never breaking my mind
by wanting to be where I am
not.

—s. mcnutt□

Stay in the Moment

We are the generation
of looking down at our cell
phones while we miss
so much beautiful life.
When was the last time
that you truly felt the wind
wrap around your skin?
When was the last time
that you really listened to
music? Not just heard
but really listened?

—s. mcnutt□

When on a date, stay
off your phone and
stay plugged into the
art of connecting.

—s. mcnutt

You always talk about
your *mistakes*—stop.
There are no mistakes.
All we have are lessons
and information about
what has happened or
is happening.

—s. mcnutt

We convince ourselves
that there is a right way
and a wrong way to live,
and there's not. There is
only reality and fantasy.
There is only what is and
what we hope it to be.
The more we live in
reality, the better off we
will be.

—s. mcnutt

Society has conditioned us to
believe that we need to always
live in the future, that we need to
always be planning and reaching
for something that we don't have.
Let's reject that. There is nothing
wrong with staying present and
remaining grateful for what we
have today.

—s. mcnutt☐

Work hard but
know when it's
time to rest.

—s. mcnutt

Working all the time
with no breaks,
without recharging
is silly. Self-care is
about recovery too.
Give yourself time
off so you can reset.

—s. mcnutt□

While society tries to
convince us that the only way
is to obsess about work and
wanting more,
I am a part of the crazy
collective who will tell you to
obsess about self-awareness,
mental health, deep
connections, love, and
sustained happiness.

—s. mcnutt☐

Most people fail because they
do not plan. They do not
execute when they do plan,
and they quit as soon as
something gets hard. I plan to
continue to plan, to follow
through with massive action,
and to persevere during tough
times. This is the blueprint
for success that I am
following until I no longer
breathe.

—s. mcnutt☐

When you spend so
much time thinking
about who you might
be in the future, all
you give yourself is
anxiety and uncertainty.

Stay in the moment
and focus on today.
Take time to create
your future, but never
obsess about the story
lines of tomorrow.

—s. mcnutt

After you've been
broken so much, you
find this surreal inner
strength—a strength
that always allows
you to put yourself
back together.

—s. mcnutt □

A Letter on Anxiety

I used to deal with crippling anxiety, and here's what I did to get rid of it. I accepted that I used to try to control every detail about an environment. I would run if it felt challenging. And that's when I realized that the feeling of anxiety makes you feel like everything is challenging, but I knew my mind was stronger, and so I ran face first into situations. It was scary at first, but the more I did it, the more comfortable I became. And then I realized that anxiety was all in my head, and it's been gone ever since that day.

With compassion,

Sylvester McNutt III

I dealt with abandonment issues
when I was younger. I would beg the
wrong people to stay, and I would
fight to keep people who didn't
want to be kept, all because I didn't
want to be alone. I didn't want to face
myself. After I healed, grew, and
became comfortable with myself, I
realized something so powerful:
those who want to be around will,
and those who do not will run for the
hills. Now I build with who wants to
stay, and I help them pack if they
want to go.

—s. mcnutt□

A Letter on Letting Them Go

□

Don't you dare break your back anymore
carrying the weight of people who do
not desire to be carried—people who
want to run for the hills and escape you.
If they want to live life without you, let
them go. Let them be free. Make sure
you always do your best with people
while they're around you, but even your
best won't be good enough for some
people, and that's okay. When they want
to run, don't feel like you need to
internalize all the pain like everything is
your fault and like there are a million
things wrong with you. Never take it
personally, because they have a choice,
and if they want to go, they should be
allowed to go.

—s. mcnutt□

The Moment You Want to Snap On Someone, Don't

Anger gets us. We feel pain that
we know damn well we didn't
deserve to feel, and of course, we
want revenge. We want them to
feel what we are feeling. Don't
do it. Don't get even. Don't
retaliate. Don't get petty. Adjust,
change, adapt, and figure out a
new plan moving forward.
Maybe it's time to cut ties—to
put your foot down—or maybe
you just need to show them that
they cannot control your
emotions with theirs. Don't snap.
Keep a level head and walk away.

—s. mcnutt

We just saw a movie on Christmas Eve.
While walking to our car, I overheard a
conversation. A group of homeless men
were laughing and teasing one another.
The one on the ground looked up at the
other and said, "I know you haven't
eaten today. Please, just take my tacos.
It's steak, bro. I know you love steak."
With a tear in his eye and a smile on his
face, the man accepted the tacos from
the other man. It was at that moment that
I realized I didn't deserve to complain or
be ungrateful ever again in my life. This
moment taught me that even when you
have nothing, you still have everything.

—s. mcnutt☐

If It's Not Genuine, Keep It Away

I retired from dealing
with the fake version
of people. I only want
your authentic self,
no matter how dark
or deep it is. I don't
expect perfect from
myself or you, but I
do expect real. I do
expect honest.

—s. mcnutt☐

Is it genuine? If
so, feed me more.

—s. mcnutt☐

A Letter to Myself on Anger

Oh dear anger, it's so good to meet you again. Sarcasm at its finest. You have become my best friend lately. When I was younger, I knew you every day. In fact, I was you; you were me. As they say, we were two peas in a pod. You helped me be violent because all I knew was violence. You helped me harm myself and others.

You helped me love to be reckless. I haven't hung out with you in so long. In fact, I made you a stranger for a while, but you've found your way back into my life. I stopped letting people get to me. I stopped caring about petty, irrelevant, irrational things. I became Zen, calm, untriggered. I proactively healed and managed my pain. I took care of business, so we never hung out.

Most people fear anxiety or public speaking or talking to girls. I know people who fear death and driving and alcoholism. My biggest fear is anger; my biggest fear is you manifesting your dirty talons in my heart again.

Anger turns me into the Hulk, into a madman, into a statistic. So now that I've been hanging out with you, you're starting to feel normal again. You're starting to convince me that I should drink, which is a promise I made to myself. I promised myself I would never drink if you were around me.

Growing up with alcoholic parents is the easiest way to become an alcoholic. I mean, damn, my parents showed me that it was okay to lose your life in a bottle every night. They showed me it was okay to fall into the base of nothingness and blame

Jack Daniels. I'm not sure who my father had a better relationship with: Was it with my mother or was it with Jack? My mom cheated on my father every night with a six-pack of Miller Genuine Draft. They couldn't commit to each other, but they could commit to the sorrows at the bottom of the bottle, which then helped them commit to violence and unruliness.

This is why I don't drink when I am angry. Those people that they were are inside of me, locked deep down inside of me, and even though I've never been what I just decried, I also never want to become it. This is why I have an inconsistent relationship with alcohol. This is why I promised myself that I would never drink when I was angry. The second that I drink when I'm angry, that is the moment when I lose everything. That is when I transform into the raging beast. The mechanic who has no tools. The athlete who has no sport or team. The person who is lost in life.

With Love,

Sylvester McNutt III

Dear Anger

I'm going to pray, I'm going to
meditate, and I'm going to take
every action I can to let you die.
You don't deserve to live inside
my temple. You no longer have
power—I do. So leave. Take my
ego with you, and allow me to
have the peace that I deserve.

—s. mcnutt□

I am on the path to figuring out
monthly how to increase my
income and decrease my expenses.
I don't care to be broke, to be
struggling, or to still be figuring
things out forever. I broke up with
the mind-set of staying on the
consistent-struggle bus years ago.
I need connections who care
about financial wellness the same
as physical fitness and spiritual
understanding.

—s. mcnutt

An Open Letter to Trust Issues

Hello again. So nice to see you. So nice to have you join my life again. I've come to realize that your existence is the death of all relationships. I've never seen a relationship recover from your presence. Does it happen? I'm sure it does somewhere, but never in my world. Never in the history of my life have I seen a relationship recover to be what it was once, and that's not a pessimistic view; it's just realistic. After trust has been broken, people always change into something else. In fact, sometimes the lack of trust helps the two people create trust. Amazing how that works. Sometimes it helps people get more serious about each other, about why they're in the relationship, and about how they're going to treat each other. So you're right. No relationship is the same when trust issues creep in, but it also doesn't mean that it's over either.

With compassion,

Sylvester McNutt III□

I don't like putting all my
personal business on the
internet. It's not that I have
things to hide. That's not it.
I don't know you, internet
people, and I don't owe
anyone on the internet
anything. I'd rather keep my
real life in my real life and
just know that the internet
life is what I want you to see.

—s. mcnutt

Simple: if worrying
about your opinion
gives me anxiety,
then I mustn't worry
about your opinion.

—s. mcnutt

Grow out of feeling like every step you take needs to be liked by others. On your path to be great, others may not understand the sacrifices that you'll have to make, but you still have to do them anyways.

—s. mcnutt

Needing approval from others will always make you scared, will always make you anxious, and will never allow you to trust yourself. Empower yourself. Be willing to take a chance on you, and if others dislike you, oh well.

—s. mcnutt □

Always value your tribe.
Nothing is more important
than family, than laughing
with lovers, than making
memories that you might
forget with people you'll
always remember.

—s. mcnutt

Privacy is important.
There isn't much you
need to know about me.
I reserve that space for
a select group of people.

—s. mcnutt☐

Top-Ten Reasons Why I
Don't Care about Your Opinion

1.It has never paid any of my bills.
2.It will not be there when I am sick.
3.It does not give me orgasms.
4.It has never made me a better person.
5.It is negative and egocentric.
6.It doesn't uplift, challenge, or encourage.
7.It came from you.
8.It will not marry me or carry my casket.
9.It is not based on facts.
10.It does not determine my worth.

A Lot Can Happen in a Year

People die. You outgrow old friends
and get tired of mundane jobs. New
careers come. New friends find your
soul. But no matter what, you grow,
you lose your mind a little bit, and
most importantly, you get a little
wiser. Your circle gets smaller because
you get stricter with your energy
and time. If you're really lucky, you'll
find love inside of yourself, inside
of friends and family, and just maybe
the universe will bless you with a
lover who laughs at your lame jokes.

—s. mcnutt

TEN

KEEP LOVING

No matter what, we
have to keep loving.□

No matter what
darkness life
brings me, I will
choose the light
of love, for that
light shines the
brightest.

—s. mcnutt □

If being single causes
you inner stress, think
about this:

Who told you that
you're required to be
in a "relationship" to
feel love? Love isn't
exclusive to dating.
We feel love with
friends, family, inside
of ourselves; love is
everywhere, all the
time.

—s. mcnutt □

The art of loving yourself
means you learn to appreciate
and accept every little thing
about who you are today. You
stop judging yourself based
on who you might be and
you've made peace with who
you once were.

—s. mcnutt

Learn who you are.
Unlearn who they
told you to be.

—s. mcnutt☐

There are too
many people
who are at war
with their own
brain. Forgive
yourself and
end the war.

—s. mcnutt

You cannot win the
battle of life if you
are always at war
with yourself.
Surrender and let go
of the position that
you need to fight
yourself—you don't.

—s. mcnutt□

Everyone is allegedly
busy; however, people
make time for those
who they care about.
They make excuses
for those whom they
do not.

—s. mcnutt

It doesn't take much
to call and say, "I
didn't want anything.
Just want to say hello
and hear your voice."
That type of treatment
goes a long way.

—s. mcnutt

I hope you cultivate the
friendships that give value to
you and them. Friends who
push each other to grow, who
call each other to laugh, who
are there for each other
through the ups and the
downs. I hope you find the
friends who love to see you
smile, but they're there for
you when you need to cry.

—s. mcnutt

I want to be the kind of friend
you can count on no matter
what. I'll give you my last
cup of water, walk with you
in a storm, and swim across
an ocean if it'll make your
life better.

—s. mcnutt□

Your partner has to be your
biggest fan and vice versa.
They should celebrate your
victories as if they were their
own successes.

—s. mcnutt☐

You deserve to
be with someone
who doesn't make
you feel crazy for
being a complex
human being.

—s. mcnutt☐

Sometimes our soul
mate is sitting right
across from us
at the coffee shop,
and we never stop
to say hello.

Open up more.

—s. mcnutt

I am here to love
people, to make
others smile, to be
someone's strength
when they have
lost their own.

—s. mcnutt☐

If you want your
relationship to
last, you have to
learn to be quiet
and listen to your
partner's wants
and needs.

—s. mcnutt

When you're loved
by the wrong person,
they take the simplest
desires and make you
feel crazy for wanting
them. Never believe
that you are crazy for
wanting respect,
communication, and
some encouragement.

Those are the basics.

—s. mcnutt□

Be the type of couple
who believes in
supporting each
other's endeavors—a
couple who believes
in encouraging each
other with positive
action and talk. Life is
too short to be with
someone who is not
invested in you.

—s. mcnutt

Many people in this
generation quit way
too soon. They want
full-time results but
only put in part-time
efforts.

—s. mcnutt

When it gets this tough, most people quit, but you're not regular. You keep fighting. You keep giving it your all.

—s. mcnutt□

I know it's hard for you, stuck in a generation that doesn't care about love and connection like you. You're a conversation starter. You're the type of person who digs deep. You ask questions. Don't change that quality about you. We need more people who care about people.

—s. mcnutt□

The pain bodies from the
past will always resurface
if you do not manage them
today. Sometimes the only
way to create something
beautiful today is to learn
from the ugly thing that
destroyed you yesterday.

—s. mcnutt

Sometimes there will be people
in your life who will need you
more than you need them. When
it's your time, be there. Have
their back and do what is needed
so they can fly, but always know
when to pull back so they can
eventually spread their wings on
their own.

—s. mcnutt☐

Never fall in love
with someone's skin,
status, or money.
Fall in love with
their personality,
with their humor,
with their smile.

—s. mcnutt☐

Just because there is
love there, that
doesn't mean we have
to give every little
piece of ourselves so
others feel complete.

—s. mcnutt☐

Tough love is real love too.
Sometimes you have to say
no, and you can do that
compassionately, with grace.
Don't demean, put down,
or make your people feel like
they're less than you because
you have to say no. Also, do
not guilt yourself into
negative emotions.

—s. mcnutt

Grow a healthy
relationship. Talk
about finances, wants,
needs, goals. Support
and encourage. Work
through hard days and
touch each other daily.

—s. mcnutt☐

Four Ways to Instantly Make Your Relationship Vibrate Higher

1. Tell them deeply and genuinely why you appreciate them.

2. Thank them for their efforts to better themselves.

3. Ask them to go for a walk instead of watching TV.

4. Simply ask them "How can I love you better?"

—s. mcnutt☐

In life,
in careers,
in personal growth,
and in all types of
connections,
alignment is
everything.

—s. mcnutt

Too many people
fall victim to forcing
a connection, a
moment, or the
energy between two
people. When you
have found the right
person, the vibe flows.

—s. mcnutt☐

Fake "I Miss You" Texts

I do not want to receive "*I miss you*" texts from people who have chosen to leave my life. You don't deserve to pop back into my life or to play with my time or my emotions just because you are lonely. You're not allowed to just check on me if there is no purpose. Every action in my life now needs a purpose, and playing small talk with someone from the past just isn't on my list anymore.

—s. mcnutt☐

No matter what, never place blame or fault. Use your energy to grow, to love yourself harder, and to raise your vibration.

—s. mcnutt

Don't wait for a
perfect situation.
Find someone
who understands
loyalty like you.
A person who
doesn't give up
during the hard
times. That's as
close to perfect as
you'll ever find.

—s. mcnutt

Currently, the only thing
I care about is spending
valuable time with a few
good people. I don't need
quantity because for my
spirit, it's all about quality.
—s. mcnutt

Love me. Bring
the best out of me.
Challenge me to
grow. If not,
leave me where
you found me.

—s. mcnutt

I'm experienced
in both love and
pain. All I want
is to decrease the
pain from the past
and love hard in
my near future.

—s. mcnutt☐

I never want you
to feel incomplete
as my lover.
Teach me how to
hold you, how to
make you smile,
and how to comfort
you when you cry.

—s. mcnutt

Be the person I
can cry with when
I'm sad or happy.
Be the person who
will allow me to
open up and be
vulnerable without
fear. Be there for
me when I can't be
there for myself,
and I promise to
return it all.

—s. mcnutt ☐

If we are apart, be
willing to listen to
the same song as me
at the same time.
Be willing to text me
a million things about
your day. Be willing
to sit on FaceTime
with me in your
underwear, even if we
aren't speaking. Just
be willing.

—s. mcnutt

Primarily I know I
will die. Before that
day comes, I simply
want to love and be
loved. Everything else
is secondary.

—s. mcnutt□

Everything in life
works out in your
favor once you take
care of yourself.
Hydrate, stretch, sleep
enough, connect with
your lover, eat healthy
food, and take care of
your mind and body,
no matter what.

—s. mcnutt

All you do is give and
give, and I hope you
know everyone in your
life is not able to thank
you. However, I thank
you. I appreciate you. I
see how hard you work
on yourself, and I see
how hard you smile when
you make other people
happy. On behalf of
everyone who is in your
life, including me,
thank you.

—s. mcnutt☐

ELEVEN

HEALING

These final reminders are short poems, thoughts,
and ideas rooted in healing—words you
can always refer to when you don't have
much time, but you crave some healing words.

I hope you approach healing as a process and not as
a button. I hope you know that no matter how well
you think you're doing, no matter how much
greatness you've manifested, healing is always a
part of any growing process. Never feel like you are
too good or above self-care, self-love, or reseting
your life.□

Healing requires
patience; healing
is a process, not
a light switch.

—s. mcnutt☐

Drink more water.
Water heals you,
and if you don't
like the taste, add
lemon, cucumber,
mint, or lime.

—s. mcnutt☐

If I try and fail,
it's okay. I want
to live fully and
die empty.

—s. mcnutt☐

You have to fail
in order to succeed.
It's a part of the
process of fulfilling
your dreams.

—s. mcnutt☐

She's a healer,
a giver. She will
nurse you back
to health when
you are sick.

—s. mcnutt☐

If you take care of
me while I am sick
you will always
hold special place
in my heart.

—s. mcnutt☐

Don't drink alcohol
just because of peer
pressure or society.
If you want tea,
water, or juice, drink
that and don't
conform to what
everyone else is
doing.

—s. mcnutt☐

I challenge
you to drink
less alcohol
and drink
more tea.

—s. mcnutt☐

I challenge
you to care
about your
health more
and your
social status
less.

—s. mcnutt

Alcohol consumption
and drugs make you
vibrate lower. Try to
limit or eliminate
them all together.

—s. mcnutt☐

Alcohol lowers your
inhibitions, which is
your ability to
rationalize a good
decision from a bad
one. Raise your
vibration and drink
less. Never drink past
your limit, or just
avoid the entire scene.

—s. mcnutt□

Vibrate Higher

Don't use alcohol
to cope with pain.
Instead, make some
tea and journal.
Go talk to someone.
Go to the gym. Do
not turn to alcohol
when you are mad,
sad, or in pain. It
will ruin you.

—s. mcnutt□

Vibrate Higher

Make sure you know
the difference
between binge
drinking and social
drinking. The former
makes you wild and
unruly, and causes
you to vibrate lower.
The latter is
considered normal
and can be healthy if
used in moderation.

—s. mcnutt□

Healing is a bath,
two glasses of
wine, a good book,
and candlelight
dancing on the
walls as you relax
and self-care.

—s. mcnutt

There are some
people you have
hurt. Call them.
Apologize. Be
accountable for
the pain you caused.

—s. mcnutt

If I ever hurt you,
I am sorry. In my
past, I was younger
and dumber. I wasn't
aware of how my
actions could've
affected people.

I will be better for
you and every person
I come across.

—s. mcnutt□

Sylvester McNutt III

When you wake up avoid
the cellphone. Get some
water, stretch, spend time
alone. Do what you have
to do to create the proper
energy needed to seize
the day.

—s. mcnutt☐

Some of your friends and
family members are low
vibrational. Don't commit
to entertaining them due
to blind loyalty. Sometimes
you have to just go away
and save yourself.

—s. mcnutt☐

266

Hanging out with the unlucky, the unhappy, the angry, and the unruly will always make you vibrate lower.

—s. mcnutt☐

Vibrate higher and distance yourself from these friendships that offer consistent struggle and pain.

—s. mcnutt☐

Sometimes your purpose
is to be the best teammate
and co-star. Help them.
Grow with them. Take
whatever role you must
in order for the team to
get a victory.

—s. mcnutt□

The best kind of teammates
pick each other up when one
falls, they push each other to
be great, and they have each
other's back until it's all over.

—s. mcnutt□

Stop chasing
communication
from adults who
claim to be your
friends but never
call or text back.
We are all busy,
but even still, busy
is no longer an
excuse.

—s. mcnutt

Fact: people make
time for people
they care about.

—s. mcnutt□

Take time out
of your night
to stretch,
to read,
to heal.

—s. mcnutt□

The problem is that
most people do not
have time
management skills.
Everyone has time,
that can no longer be
the excuse.

—s. mcnutt□

Some of us
will never
heal because
we eat
poisonous
food.

—s. mcnutt□

Music has the
ability to heal
you, to help
you feel
understood.

—s. mcnutt□

If I send you a song,
it is because the music
made me think about
you, or even deeper,
it's helping me explain
who I am to you in a
way that I cannot.

—s. mcnutt☐

Vibrate higher by
paying attention
to the energy that
the music you
listen to carries.
Sometimes it builds,
and other times
it destroys.

—s. mcnutt☐

Corporate America,
in some cases,
creates toxic
environments that
will get you sick.
Sometimes you
must leave these
places to heal.

—s. mcnutt□

You have sick and
planned days off
for a reason.
Use them to focus
on healing, on
recovery, and on the
fun things that
you care about.

—s. mcnutt□

Don't stay in a
job environment
if it kills your joy,
your identity, and
your happiness.

Find your purpose.

—s. mcnutt

You can get money a
lot of ways and from
many different sources.
Don't stay stuck in a
place just because of
money. If it hurts, if it
drains, if it causes
depression, there are
other routes.

—s. mcnutt☐

When I get sick, I go
away from the world.
I don't work; I don't
school; I go back to
the basics and focus
on healing. Everyone
deserves the best of
me, including me, so
excuse me while I
take time to heal.

—s. mcnutt

Employers think
calling out means
you're sick with the
cold or flu, but that's
only physical. Mental
health is a thing too,
and if my mind is not
right, I will not suffer
and fake happiness on
that day. I will call out
so I can heal and
come back better.

—s. mcnutt☐

Going to a job every
day that I didn't love
made me sick. I did
what I had to do for
as long as I had to do
it, and then one day
I woke up. I saw that
it's better to do
something you like,
even if that means
less money, than
staying at a job you
hate for more money.

—s. mcnutt☐

Pay more attention
to fun, to hobbies,
to rest, to things
that spark you.
School and work
will always be
calling you, so
see what else
life has to offer.

—s. mcnutt☐

Put the cell phone
down more. Doing
this allows you to see
people's lies on your
timeline less.

—s. mcnutt□

A lot of people lie
on social media about
who they are because
they have no idea who
they might be. Don't
be a lot of people.
You're not perfect,
you're not always
right, and there is no
reason to pretend
otherwise.

—s. mcnutt□

Never create a
perfect image of
yourself. It will
make you sick
when you want
to be imperfect
or real. Show your
scars and your flaws,
and most importantly,
show that you
embrace all of you.

—s. mcnutt

I don't show all of my
personal life on social
media for two reasons:
I like important and
special moments to stay
private, and none of you
will be here to help me
build my life if everything
falls apart. Stop acting
like I owe you anything.

—s. mcnutt□

You can instantly heal
your life by stopping the
process of putting all your
business on social media.
Move in private, let
people guess, and allow
your real friends to know
the truth.

—s. mcnutt☐

Healing is getting rid of
people or behaviors that
have caused you to get
sick.

—s. mcnutt☐

Healing is a formula.

Add what heals.
Subtract what hurts.
Learn from what goes.
Cherish what stays.

—s. mcnutt□

Be patient while
you shed old skin
and while new
layers grow.

—s. mcnutt□

Dear Society,

Fuck you for laughing at people who need to cry aloud. We will no longer suffer in silence.

—s. mcnutt□

I have no shame in saying *I don't know*. I have no shame in asking for help after I have failed. I have no problem asking for more explanation. I want to learn.

—s. mcnutt□

Never be afraid to
seek help from a
counselor, teacher,
health professional,
friend, or even a
stranger. Don't hold
everything in.

—s. mcnutt☐

I hope my kids feel
like I am a beacon
of support and
encouragement.

—s. mcnutt☐

I do not see the value in
spanking, hitting, or beating
children. A true master of
communication can connect
with a child.

Many adults are mad at their
children because the child
mimics behavior that he or
she saw from the parents.

How can we beat something
that came from us for acting
like us?
—s. mcnutt

You can discipline
children without
hitting them, without
screaming at them like
you hate them.

—s. mcnutt☐

We will make many
mistakes as parents,
but we should all
have one goal:

create an experience
for our children that
they do not have to
heal from.

—s. mcnutt□

Become fully aware
of your inner
dialogue. The key to
true healing occurs
in between those
conversations you
have with yourself.

—s. mcnutt□

Becoming truly conscious of your thoughts doesn't mean that you're never negative or down. It means you identify it quickly. It means you work through the low vibrational energy and move forward.

—s. mcnutt☐

To truly heal your life, make meditation a part of your daily routine. Practice silence—not speaking or obsessively thinking. Remain in a state of being and allow everything to flow.

—s. mcnutt☐

If you have trouble
clearing your mind,
that means you need
to practice a session
of mindfulness today.

Pause your brain.
Stop obsessing
about thoughts,
things you
need to do,
assignments, or
deadlines. Sit still
and breathe deeply
with the
intention of truly
becoming one with
your breath.

—s. mcnutt□

If there is one thing
that you can do right
now to add more
healing to your life,
what would you
guess it might be?

*No, stalking your
ex's social media
is not the answer.*

It's called meditation
—breathing deeply
with the intent of
becoming one with
the moment.

—s. mcnutt□

Have you ever disliked
or loved someone as soon
as you met them?

Of course you have.

Your proof that
vibrational energies
are real and the energy
we carry daily matters.

—s. mcnutt☐

The drama queen or king you know always says that they don't want drama, but they unconsciously keep triggering dramatic situations because that is the vibrational energy they are giving out. The universe is only matching what is already inside of them.

—s. mcnutt

Healing from the pain is not easy, you're right, *but it is possible to hea*l. And that hope is all I need to know to keep smiling, to keep laughing, and to keep telling myself that everything is going to be okay.
–s. mcnutt□

This was a tough
pill to swallow,
but once I did,
I healed. I grew.
I vibrated higher.

Your success or
your failure is 100
percent on you, on
your effort, on your
mind-set,
on your behaviors.

—s. mcnutt☐

Gratitude allows
you to vibrate
higher. It allows
you to keep what
you have. It allows
you to water the
plants that have
already grown
from your
majestic garden.

—s. mcnutt☐

Don't obsess
about what you
don't have. Look
at what you've lost.
Learn from it, and
remain forever
grateful for what
you do have.

—s. mcnutt☐

In some cases,
wanting more
is a disease.
Heal yourself
by cultivating
a consistent
space of
gratefulness.

—s. mcnutt☐

Keep it simple: stop
buying things that
do not enhance
your life.

—s. mcnutt

Investments

The mission is to
practice investing:
invest financially,
save money, increase
your income, invest in
your health and
well-being, save energy,
and increase
your happiness.

—s. mcnutt☐

Don't forget to
unplug from the
cell phone, from
social media,
from television,
from other people's
opinions. There is
a lot of value in
reconnecting with
your inner world.

—s. mcnutt☐

The cell phone is
the most powerful and
the most dangerous
tool of our generation.
Use it wisely; do not
use it aimlessly.

—s. mcnutt☐

You will heal
your sleep schedule
if you stay off
your cell phone
and computer at
least thirty to forty
minutes before
it's time to rest.

—s. mcnutt□

You can heal your
peace of mind by
turning notifications
off on your cell phone.
Keeping them on
always pulls your
attention away from
the present moment.

—s. mcnutt□

Heal your brain from the addiction that society has given us. Be intentional about going hours upon hours without checking your cell phone.

—s. mcnutt□

Sometimes you need to leave your cell phone at home on purpose. Go to school, work, or to the gym with the intention to be fully alert, completely immersed in the present moment.

—s. mcnutt□

We are at a point in society
where people will say that
they *need* their phones.
This is a false claim. You
need air, water, sleep, love,
and belonging—human
connection. If you go a few
hours without your phone,
you will survive.

—s. mcnutt□

Breaking Cellphone Addiction

I took notifications
off, all email, all
games and useless
apps, all social media
apps, and anything
that constantly goes
off. I keep sounds off
and brightness down.
This all helped me.

□s□mcnutt□

I care deeply about
human connection.
I desire to cultivate
and sustain
stimulating
conversation,
intriguing interaction,
and new experiences.

—s. mcnutt□

When people talk to
you, put your phone
down and look them
in the eye. Give
feedback and engage
in conversation. The
time line and text
messages will always
be there.

—s. mcnutt□

More people need to
understand that scrolling
your phone aimlessly
when other humans are
trying to communicate is
nonverbal feedback that
tells them you're uninterested
in connecting with them.

—s. mcnutt

In the generation of *phone
in my hand*, I respect anyone
who can put it away and
engage, people who crave
human connection like I do.

— s. mcnutt□

I challenge you to set aside time each day to cultivate "cell phone–free time." Time to stretch, to read, to write, to draw, to paint, to lift, to swim, to go for a hike, to do anything other than scrolling vibes.

—s. mcnutt☐

If it brings you constant stress and discomfort, please understand this: it is trying to teach you something.

—s. mcnutt☐

Fall in love with taking care
of yourself. Fall in love with
the path of deep healing. Fall in
love with becoming the best
version of yourself but with
patience, with compassion and
respect to your own journey.

—s. mcnutt☐

Promise yourself that
after you read this you
will breakup with
self-sabotage, you will
stop talking down to
yourself, and you will
try your hardest to
breathe and let some
things go.

—s. mcnutt☐

You have survived the worst already, you are still here winning, and fighting. Just keep loving, be patient with healing, and lead with love and joy.

—s.mcnutt

Be less serious and have more fun. Think more about the moment and less about the future or past. The main thing you need more of in your life, is more happiness, and you deserve it too.

—s. mcnutt□

Trust the vibes
you get; energy doesn't lie.

—s. mcnutt

Energy is everything
and it is everywhere.
It's in the food you eat,
the music you listen to,
and the people you
surround yourself with.
Always pay attention
to energy.
—s. mcnutt□

Thank you for reading
Care Package: A Path To Deep Healing.

I dedicate this to us. We have been through a lot but we are recovering, we are loving, and we are fighting for us and those around us. Our main goal should be to focus on getting rid of the pain, and we know it's not *easy*, but it is possible. I hope *Care Package* showed you and brought you words that make you believe that. Healing from the pain is not easy, you're right, but it is possible to heal. And that hope is all I need to know to keep smiling, to keep laughing, and to keep telling myself that everything is going to be okay. I am thankful that you allowed *Care Package* to assist you on this journey. Please take the time to reflect, to write, to travel, to do whatever is going to allow you to marinate with your own energy. Take a day off of work or school to sit in nature if it will allow you to figure things out. Stay inspired and stay motivated. Lastly, I need your help too. Please go leave a positive review for the *Care Package* book on amazon.com and any other site that you visit. Reviews help me, the self-published author, find new readers. Your review could save someone's life, so please, do it as soon as possible. I love you all so much. I love you because you put yourself first today, thank you.

with compassion,

Sylvester McNutt III

Chronological order of my entire self-published library, available exclusively on www.sylvestermcnutt.net

The Accelerated: Success Is A Choice (2012)

Dear Queen Journey: A Path To Self Love (2014)

Dear Soul: Love After Pain (2015)

Dear Love Life: Efficient Dating in The Technology Era (2016)

This Is What Real Love Feels Like (2016)

Lust For Life (2017)

Care Package: A Path To Deep Healing (2018)

CPSIA information can be obtained
at www.ICGtesting.com
Printed in the USA
BVHW07s1931050718
520889BV00002B/2/P